How Audio Works

Vincent Musolino

ISBN-13: 978-1535364034

To my wife.

List of Contents

Alternate List of Contents

Disclaimer

I decline any liability for any injury and/or damage to persons or property which might be caused by improper use or operation of material present in this book.

(You never know)

Cover photo credits

Preface

When I started to get interested in audio eight years ago, I started from scratch. I knew nothing about any of it, so I began to absorb anything I could find on the topic - some of the sources are listed in the Appendix A.

I decided to write down, in my own words, what I found important in my journey to a better understanding of audio. I listened to podcasts and read books and forum posts from people who knew much more than I did - or at least made me frown and jot down a question so that I could go back and verify the answer later. And before long, what started as a bunch of lines in a Word document grew into a much larger than anticipated collection of explanations, figures and tables.

As this document grew, I decided to focus on two things: first, I wanted to explain the basic technical audio stuff: is there a difference between a volume knob on a speaker and a gain knob on a preamp? How does a microphone work? How can my ears detect multiple frequencies at the same time? What the heck is impedance and should I care? Do I seriously need to put blankets up the walls in my living room? Second, because audio is technical, people feel compelled to use jargon, so I tried to reference as many cabalistic terms as possible: part of the initiation ritual in audio circles is to understand what is meant by "adding 2 dB at 300 on the 1073". Therefore, I have added equipment tables and a large index of terms.

Finally, I am completely ignoring entire library sections worth of content about audio. If it is not in here, it is simply because I was not interested in it. The idea was to have a short reference book anyway, not an Audio Codex (pun intended) of 667 pages – someone already tried.

My gratitude goes to Christophe, Enzo and Fabien who have helped me write this book by reviewing it; their invaluable work helped me gain a different perspective on the book before sending it out – much like what you do with a music mix, really.

Finally, many thanks to the people I have listened to, talked to or read from. Writing this book would have been impossible 20 years ago, in the Dark Ages of Paper and Telephone.

Thank you, interwebz.

Introduction

This book is intended for music fans of all sorts and ages.

Whether a musician who wants to understand the engineering behind the music, a hobbyist who wants to start recording their songs, a music lover who wants to understand why certain records sound the way they do, an audio engineer who wants to make sure they can nail the basic technicalities of their craft, or simply someone eager to learn the basics of audio engineering, this book is for you.

The title of the book is "How Audio Works". The problem is that audio gets hard quickly. This book aims at making the fundamentals of audio easier to understand, but it still is a challenging task that requires some thinking. Because audio is an engineering discipline, there will be math. Simple functions, simple equations, but math nonetheless. Even if I tried to avoid mathing you out, it is the basic language of engineering. Understanding the equations is not required to understand the principles behind them, but it helps.

I decided to organize the book in the most intuitive way possible: follow the sound from its creation to its rendering, from the vibrating string to the sound in your ears. Chapter 1 deals with physical sound and its description in terms of waves. Chapter 2 explains how the sound is transformed and transported by a series of devices (microphones, cables, amplifiers, etc.) from the analog physical domain to the digital virtual domain. Chapter 3 describes the basic transformative operations available in the digital domain. Chapter 4 explains how the sound is transformed back into the analog domain and how we humans detect it.

Appendix A contains a list of sources; on that topic, I have removed all the Wikipedia references I had originally included: if a term of concept is not clear, there is a good chance that there is some Wikipedia article about it because, well, you and I are not the first ones to ponder the issue; if there is no article, call me. Appendix B is a short compendium to help the non-engineers make sense of the multiple units used in the book. Appendix C is a detailed Glossary so that technical terms can be quickly found and understood throughout the book. Appendix D contains the complete list of tables, figures and equations.

Ready to jump in?

Chapter 1. Physical Sound

1.1. Sound Waves

What are sound waves?

Sound waves are air molecules vibrating under the influence of an initial shock: a string being plucked; a drum head being hit. Any movie with loud explosions in outer space should have their technical staff flogged in public: there are no air molecules in space; no air means no sound.

The movement of the string displaces the air molecules around it; these air molecules form alternating zones of higher and lower pressure. When we say that sound is propagating, we mean that those zones are propagating; the air molecules themselves do not move. If a sensitive membrane (e.g. a microphone) is put in front of the sound source, it will feel those alternating zones of higher and lower pressure as alternating moments of higher and lower pressure.

How do we represent them?

The best way to represent this type of behavior is with an oscillating function, going from some lower boundary measuring troughs in pressure to some higher boundary measuring peaks in pressure, with at some point in the middle values which represent the average pressure felt by the measuring device (see Figure 1).

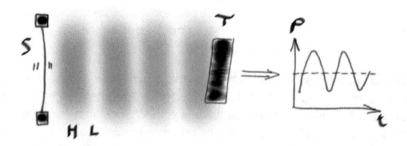

Figure 1 Sound Waves *A string S vibrates, creating mobile high (H) and low (L) air pressure areas; this can be represented by a sine wave like function of pressure (P) versus time (t); the device T feels the varying pressure; why T? Read on.*

In a simple one-dimensional case, the sound pressure wave P as a function of its location x and the time t takes the form of a sine function:

$$P(x,t) = A * \sin\left[2 * \Pi\left(\frac{x}{\lambda} - v * t\right)\right]$$

Equation 1 Sine Wave

where A is the wave's *amplitude*, describing how large or small it can be, v (Greek letter "nu") is the *frequency*, λ (Greek letter "lambda") is the wave's *wavelength* (see Equation 2); $2 * \Pi * x / \lambda$ is sometimes represented by the symbol Φ (Greek letter "phi") and is called the wave's *phase*. P represents the pressure recorded at a certain time t by the microphone which is located at the x position.

What is a wavelength?

The wavelength λ represents the distance between two points of the function which have the same characteristics, for example two peaks or two troughs. The frequency v can be obtained with the following formula which is valid in air (linear medium) but not in water (dispersive medium):

$$v = \frac{c}{\lambda}$$

Equation 2 Wavelength and Frequency

where c is the speed of sound; sound travels at roughly 113 feet per second / 343 meters per second at 20° Celsius / 68° Fahrenheit. A linear medium (like air) is a medium in which the waves with different frequencies all travel at the same speed; in a dispersive medium (like water), the waves with different frequencies travel at different speeds; the sound gets progressively deformed as it moves.

What are frequencies?

Frequencies are measured in Hertz (Hz) and wavelengths in meters (m). Examples of typical wavelengths and corresponding frequencies can be found in the next table.

The lowest frequency a human ear can hear is called the *human hearing threshold* (more on that in Section 4.4); its value is 20 Hz and is represented by a wave of length 17 m, while the highest frequency a human ear can hear is 20 kHz (17 mm length).

Wavelength	Frequency
1 m	343 Hz
1 ft.	1.12 kHz
17 m = 56 ft.	**20 Hz**
17 mm = 0.67 in.	**20 kHz**
0.78 m = 31 in.	**A (440 Hz)**
1.31 m = 4 ft. 4 in.	**C4 (261 Hz)**

Table 1 Typical Wavelengths and Frequencies

Standard tuning with the A note at 440 Hz is 0.78 m long while the middle C on a piano is 1.31 meters long. Again, note that air molecules do not travel with sound; they literally oscillate in place in the direction of the sound, which is why sound waves are longitudinal waves and why there is wind coming with them. What does move in the direction of the sound are pressure changes caused by those vibrating air molecules.

1.2. Sound Volume

Sound volume is always measured with respect to some reference level and almost never in absolute terms like most other quantities are. Thus, what we think of as "sound volume" is in fact a ratio in sound pressure. The unit measuring sound pressure is the *Bel*. Because we want to be able to pick out small pressure ratio differences, we do not use the Bel, but the decibel (symbol: *dB*): $1\ dB = 0,1\ Bel$.

What is the decibel scale?
Since the dB is a relative scale, we need a reference. The softest sound a human can hear is defined as 0 dB *SPL* (equivalent to air pressure of 20 µPa) where *SPL* stands for *Standard Pressure Level*. Because sound pressure ratios span over a very large range of values, the dB scale is logarithmic; this means that the space between 1 and 10 is the same as the space between 10 and 100; this allows displaying much larger scales in a convenient manner (see Table 2 below). The choice of a logarithmic scale also has a physiological reason: the ear itself has logarithmic sensitivity.

The equation linking the sound wave amplitude ratio r with the pressure ratio I (in dB) is defined as:

$$I = 10 * log_{10}r^2 = 20 * log_{10}r$$

Equation 3 Sound and Intensity Amplitude Ratios

How does that work? Imagine a pressure ratio r of 100000 (one hundred thousand); since $100000 = 10^5$, the log function is 5 and the decibel value will be 20 * 5 = 100 dB.

For example, if the pressure ratio at some location is one thousand times larger than that at some other location, we will say that there is a sixty-decibel difference; if the pressure ratio is twice as high, there is a six-decibel difference. Conversely, if the pressure ratio is half, we will say that there is a negative six decibel difference: the logarithmic scale transforms multiplication and division into addition and subtraction.

Air pressure ratio r	Intensity ratio I
$100000 = 10^5$	100 dB
$10000 = 10^4$	80 dB
$1000 = 10^3$	60 dB
$100 = 10^2$	40 dB
$10 = 10^1$	20 dB
~2	6 dB
1	0 dB
~0.5	-6 dB
$0.1 = 10^{-1}$	-20 dB
$0.01 = 10^{-2}$	-40 dB
$0.001 = 10^{-3}$	-60 dB
$0.0001 = 10^{-4}$	-80 dB
$0.00001 = 10^{-5}$	-100 dB

Table 2 Amplitude Ratios and Their dB Equivalent

1.3. Phase and Polarity

Polarity and phase are usually confused with each other, but they are not the same. The phase is the initial value of the wave when $t = 0$: it is related to the time axis of the wave; polarity, on the other hand, is related to the displacement axis of the sine wave x and represents the sign of the sine wave (see Equation 1).

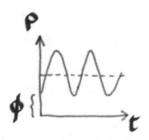

Figure 2 Phase and Polarity *The pressure sine function has the value*
Φ at t = 0; because it is positive, it has positive polarity.

What does switching polarity mean?
You will hear people talking (correctly) about *switching the polarity* of an audio signal; it means changing the sign of the signal. Some people (incorrectly) say "Switching the phase of the signal"; they mean switching the polarity, but their mistake is almost logical: for sine waves, this is equivalent to changing the phase by 180 degrees since two sine waves out of phase by 180° (π) will cancel out[1]. Note that two signals can be in phase but of opposite polarity and of course perfectly cancel each other out; that is in fact the only way to cancel two signals.

What does "checking the phase" mean?
In audio terminology, "checking for phase coherence" or "*checking the phase*" means making sure that all waveforms stemming from recorded instruments roughly have peaks (or nulls) at the same time so that sound does not cancel out. This is used after recording an instrument to make sure that the signals do not cancel each other; this typically could happen when recording drums with multiple microphones: if the recorded sounds are of opposite polarity, some of their frequencies could cancel each other out, making the sound thinner. This can be very difficult to pull off, especially with multiple sound sources; the best result is achieved by listening to the different sources, switching polarity of each source in turn, and selecting the result with the best sound.

---

[1] $\sin(x) + \sin(x + \pi) = \sin(x) - \sin(x) = 0$

1.4. Harmonics

What is a harmonic?

When an instrument is played or a note sang, different frequencies are generated: the *fundamental frequency* (or fundamental note) and *overtones*, also called *harmonics*. The basic reason why this happens is because a vibrating string (attached at both ends) has very precise ways of vibrating to accommodate for the physical constraints of the system (the string material, how the ends are fixed and the medium in which it vibrates: air, water, etc.). These different ways are "modes" which possess unique points with zero vibration on the string called "nodes". The number of these nodes tells you what harmonic we are talking about.

What is an octave?

Octaves happen every time the number of nodes is a power of 2: 1 (because $2^0=1$), 2, 4, 8, 16, etc. Alternatively, it can be defined as the difference in frequency between a base frequency and its double. A *semitone* (or *half-step*) is defined as $1/12^{th}$ of an octave.

Node	Frequency	Overtone	Harmonic
0	440 Hz	Fundamental	First
1	880 Hz	First	Second
2	1320 Hz	Second	Third
3	1760 Hz	Third	Fourth
4	2200 Hz	Fourth	Fifth

Table 3 First Five Harmonics for Standard A

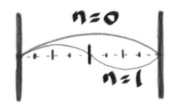

Figure 3 Harmonics The first order harmonic (n = 0) has no nodes; the second order harmonic (n = 1) has one node in the middle of the string; the next even order harmonic nodes are marked with markers of decreasing size up to fourth order harmonics. The doubling of the frequency for each subsequent octave becomes obvious.

Note that the first overtone is the second harmonic – it is only a matter of definition; they do represent the same frequency. Harmonics in between those perfect intervals become increasingly complex.

1.5. Frequencies and Instruments

In the following figure, the major music instruments (including vocal chords) are displayed, including their main frequency ranges and some commonly used terminology.

The first line (Notes) indicates the name of the note as referenced from a standard piano keyboard with 88 notes: C1 is the first C note all the way to the left of keyboard; C4 is the middle C.

The second line displays the corresponding frequencies in Hz.

Each frequency range (called Type in the figure, displayed on the fifth line) has both negative (third line) and positive (fourth line) connotations, depending on context and taste; descriptions are what they are, understand what you can ☺

The last line displays the full spectrum of human hearing (called *Standard audible range*) from 20 Hz to 20 kHz. You can test your own limits at reference [1]; my upper limit is 14 kHz, which is somewhat low.

Dark gray covers the instruments' main frequencies, while light gray is for overtones. Instrument names are displayed approximately in the middle of their frequency range: 240 Hz for male vocals, 450 Hz for female vocals.

The standard tuning note is *Standard A*, at 440 Hz, which corresponds to the middle of the range for pianos and female vocals. Coincidence?

Note that trained ears can hear a difference in *pitch* (frequency) of a note of 1-2 cents; a *cent* is 1% of the difference between 2 adjacent semitones. If you hear someone saying "She is off by a couple of cents", they mean that the singer's note is off pitch by 2% in the frequency range of that semitone; if she is singing a standard A at 440 Hz, 2% is 8.8 Hz; if she is singing a high A at 880 Hz, she is 17.6 Hz off. You can test your own sensitivity at [2]; I am 90% for 5 cents at 440 Hz, which is decent.

Many of the instruments on the chart have their middle range below 1 kHz; however, much of the magic in making music happens way beyond that frequency – try to use a low pass filter (see Section 2.5) with a cutoff frequency of 1 kHz and you will see why.

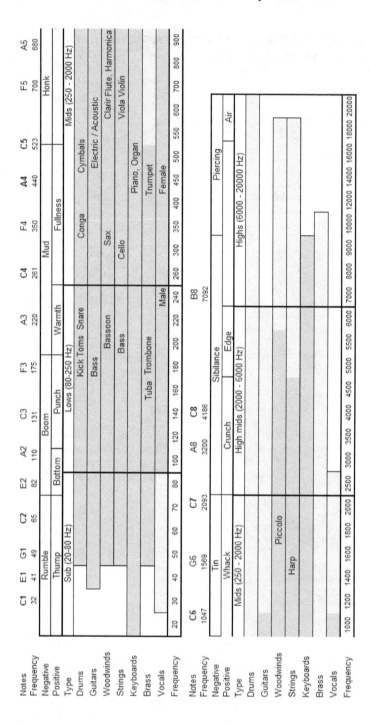

Figure 4 Summarized Frequency Chart

Chapter 2. From Analog Sound to Digital Audio

2.1. Signal Chain

What does analog mean?

A sound generated by an instrument takes the form of an analog pressure wave. The term *analog* refers to the fact that the pressure varies continuously with some variable, for example the string motion; this is by contrast with a *digital* signal that varies in discrete steps, for example the binary code representing the different voltages encoding the air pressure.

Right now, we are still in the analog domain. If we want to record (or *track*) this sound, this varying air pressure, we must use a device called a *transducer*: it captures one form of energy (for example. mechanical, like air pressure) and transforms it into another (for example electrical, like voltages). That is why the device capturing the varying air pressure in Figure 1 is labelled with a "T": it is a transducer.

Why do we need transducers?

Because we do not know how to encode information with air pressures, but we have found ways to use voltages instead. Since our best tool to treat information is a computer, we must transform the electrical (analog) signal into a digital signal through a *converter*. On the way out, the same thing happens: our ears are not very good at decoding electrical signals, so we transform the treated digital signal through another converter before transducing it into sound pressures for our ears' pleasure.

What is a signal chain?

The chain of devices and events depicted in Figure 5 below is called a *signal chain*. Of course, the signal chain will vary greatly depending on the situation; what is presented in Figure 5 is the most complete logical representation of a signal chain with an analog source, an analog destination and some processing in between. What takes place in that middle processing box (labelled P) depends on what needs to be achieved: improving a recording's volume so that it can be better mixed with other signals; mixing different signals so that they sound good together; slightly modifying the balance of a sound so that it sounds better in a certain listening environment.

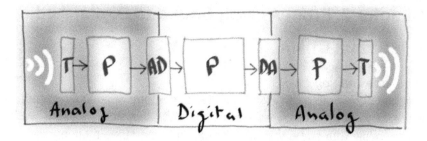

Figure 5 Signal Chain *The sound travels from left to right: a pressure wave (analog signal) is generated, then transduced (T), then processed (P), then converted into a digital signal by an analog to digital converter (AD), then processed in the digital domain (P), then converted back into an analog signal by a digital to analog converter (DA), then processed (P), then transduced (T) back into a pressure wave.*

To make the above figure more concrete, you could imagine that (from left to right) the first "T" is a microphone, the first P is a microphone pre-amplifier, the "AD" is found in an audio interface, the second P is the computer with which you will treat the sound, the "DA" is found in the same audio interface, the third "P" is a speaker amplifier and the last "T" is a set of speakers: those are the devices that you would use to record a sound with a microphone. If you do not know what all those terms mean, do not worry, each will be treated to its own section later.

Why do I need a signal chain?

But why have this processing at all? Isn't the simplest signal chain just having the source and the destination close by, like in a live performance? You are right, it is; but what if there is a spatial difference between them, for example I record the sound in one location and I want to play it 1000 miles away? Or what if I want to listen to it again? That is why we need to record sounds: to make sure they are available when we need them.

The issue is that as soon as you decide to record anything, you are in fact changing what you are recording: first by capturing only a part of the whole performance and second by playing the recording in an environment that is different from the one in which the recording was made. All of this might seem very logical and maybe a bit obvious, but those are precisely the reasons why audio engineering exists: to create or recreate a pleasant listening experience from recorded material.

What is audio engineering's job?

One debate I will put to rest right now is this: shouldn't the audio engineering's job be to reproduce the original performance with as much fidelity as possible? Since you have paid attention the last couple of lines, you already know the answer: no. It is just not possible. Fidelity to what? An ephemeral performance which ceased to exist the moment it was over? Everything is different once you have recorded the performance, so yes, music is a complete fabrication, much like movies are: I hear no one complaining about it, and gods know how much editing goes into making a movie – can you imagine a director who would have to shoot the whole movie in one go?

To simplify the signal chain displayed in Figure 5, let us imagine that the transducer in the left-hand side analog domain is the *membrane* of a microphone picking up sound from the source and that the transducer restituting the sound in the right-hand side analog domain is the *driver* of a speaker (driver is the technical term, but it is basically a membrane pushing air, see Section 4.2). The transducer on the way in could also be an electric guitar pickup, or a telephone. On the way out, the transducer could be the tiny speakers in your ear buds or the gigantic sound systems in your favorite arena, or a telephone, for that matter[2].

2.2. Microphones

What is a microphone?

An acoustic *microphone* is made of at least an electroacoustic transducer (also called *capsule*), containing the membrane or *diaphragm* mentioned earlier and a case to hold it which acts as a windshield. When the sound waves hit the microphone, it transmits its energy to the diaphragm and displaces it by tiny amounts: 4 μm (four millionth of a millimeter) at 1 kHz!

How does a microphone work?

The way a microphone then transforms this mechanical (pressure) energy into electrical energy is what determines the type of microphone; however, all microphone types function in the same manner: air molecules hit the diaphragm; those collisions make the diaphragm move; the moving diaphragm creates an electrical current by varying the electrical tension (or

---

[2] These will not be discussed here but references [3] and [4] are a good start if you are interested

voltage) in a circuit (more on that later; note that to express differences in voltages, you can use dBs as well, but the reference level and how they are measured will be different); the current is then transmitted to some device in the chain. This process is in fact a form of encoding mechanical information into electrical information. Please note that the created current varies with time; this is important because electrical components in the path of a varying or alternating current (AC) must be described not with resistance but with *impedance* as we will see in Section 2.2.

Those membranes capturing pressure changes are mechanical devices; this means that they move, they age, they resonate, etc. That is one of the reasons why audio equipment in general (microphones, microphone preamplifiers and speakers) can be very expensive: the quality of the design, the quality of the materials and the processes used to manufacture them can make a difference in the final product. Whether that difference in quality is large enough to warrant the (usually very) large difference in price, you must find out for yourself, but I have heard very respectable people say that you can make great sounding music with cheap equipment. This is a technical book about audio, but I (and many others with me) am a firm believer in the notion that the musician, the performance and the instrument (in that order) count much more in the quality of the music than the equipment.

The transformation of pressure into electricity is not instantaneous because the diaphragm has a mass which must be moved for the corresponding current to be created; this means that for very high frequencies, if the mass of the diaphragm is too large, the diaphragm will not move fast enough: it will not be sensitive to those frequencies. How quickly the diaphragm moves determines the *microphone sensitivity* , usually measured in dBV (simply another relative scale, this time to measure sensitivity in Volts per Pascal, or V/Pa: the worlds of mechanical pressure (measured in Pa) and electricity (measured in V) nicely meet in this unit!).

Microphone Types

There are three main acoustic microphone types: condenser, dynamic and ribbon. The first two read the pressure while the last one reads the difference in pressure with respect to distance – that is why ribbon microphones are sometimes called pressure gradient microphones. All three microphone types need to be amplified so that the signal is strong enough to be processed later: the output level of the microphone is called *microphone level*, while the desired processing level is called *line level*. How much amplification the microphone amplifier proposes is important because if it is not large enough, the outgoing signal's level will not be high enough.

Condenser Microphone

A capacitor is an electrical component used to store electrostatic energy; how is this useful? Well, for starters, capacitors used to be called condensers; the name stuck, even though it is technically obsolete, but they mean the same thing. Furthermore, if we want to produce electricity from sound pressure, we need a device that can vary its production depending on how much pressure is coming in. That is exactly where the capacitor comes in: the *condenser microphone*, also called *capacitor microphone*, is a microphone where one of the plates of the capacitor is the diaphragm; the air pressure variations move the diaphragm, making the capacitor larger or smaller in volume, hence modulating the tension in the circuit proportionally to the frequency of the air pressures changes, in turn representing the frequency of the originating sound.

What is phantom power?

One of the reasons why the condenser microphone needs a source of energy to properly function is the fact that the incoming voltage variations due to the varying sound pressure only module an existing voltage; this source of energy is called *phantom power*. The other reason is that most of the time, the condenser microphone needs an amplification of its signal close to the source of electricity to prevent loss of certain frequencies due to electrical effects (see Section 2.2). I say most of the time because another type of condenser called the electret condenser has special material inserted between the diaphragm and the capacitor back plate so that the outside energy source is only needed to operate the amplifier. Condensers are known to reproduce high frequencies very well because of their design: their diaphragms are very light and move quickly under air pressure.

How do we categorize condenser microphones?

Condenser microphones are sometimes categorized by the size of the diaphragm. *Small diaphragm condensers* (*SDCs*) tend to have their diaphragm to be less than 1 inch / 2.5 cm in diameter[3], *large diaphragm*

---

[3] See [3] and [5]

condensers (*LDCs*) covering the rest of the range. The different advantages and disadvantages of using LDCs and SDCs along with the explanation of why they behave differently are covered in details in [6], but there is a trade-off between sensitivity and fidelity. Fidelity, especially at high frequencies, comes with smaller lighter diaphragms, while sensitivity comes with larger diaphragms. That is because larger diaphragms have a higher capacitive reactance (it is proportional to the volume of the condenser) and thus a lower impedance, which means a lower sensitivity (see Section 2.2). SDCs are mainly used when high fidelity at high frequencies is desired and the loss of sensitivity is not too much of an issue; LDCs are mainly used in the opposite case of high sensitivity and lower requirements in fidelity.

Condenser microphones can also be categorized by how the original electric signal is amplified: via a *tube* (or a valve), or via a field effect transistor (*FET*). Much like for guitar amplifiers, the different components have an impact on the final sound because they modify the electrical path through which the voltage-encoded sound information transits. Without going into details, tube amplifiers are thought to add pleasing harmonics to the captured sound and distort the sound better when pushed to the limit of their capabilities; you will hear engineers talk about a "tube sound" for guitar amplifiers and microphones, for example. Whether you care or not is up to your ears (and your budget, as always).

Dynamic Microphone

The *dynamic microphone*, also called *moving-coil microphone*, uses induction to create an electrical current when the diaphragm (under varying air pressure from the sound) moves a magnet with a coil of wire wound around it. The larger the move, the larger the induced electrical current. Because its transducing system (diaphragm + magnet + coil) is much heavier than that of a condenser microphone, the dynamic microphone cannot reproduce high frequencies like the condenser can. However, it is more rugged, sturdier, and does not need phantom power to operate since there is no component which needs power inside the microphone.

Ribbon Microphone

The *ribbon microphone*, also called *velocity microphone*, contains a thin corrugated (wrinkled, or bent into folds) metal foil, usually aluminum, placed in a magnetic field, which will move around under changing air pressure. The ribbon acts like a coil and uses the induction phenomenon to create the current, exactly like the dynamic microphone. Because the coil only has one turn, the output voltage is smaller than for the condenser and dynamic microphone, making amplification an absolute must. Also, the ribbon being very thin (in the micron range µm), ribbon microphones are more fragile than their two counterparts. Recent designs and ribbon materials have made ribbon microphone sturdier, but it is still not recommended to put them in front of a kick or a snare drum! Older ribbon microphone designs did not incorporate amplifiers and did not require phantom power to operate; worse, phantom power could damage the ribbon with an overcharge. More recent models now incorporate an internal amplifier to be used with phantom power.

Sound Pickup Patterns

What is a pickup pattern?
Microphones, depending on their capsule design, can capture air pressure coming from certain areas better than from others. For example, ribbon microphones can pick up sound from the front and rear because the ribbon is exposed to sound waves on both of its sides. A condenser microphone is directional in nature since sound pushes on the diaphragm from only one direction. Of course, microphone manufacturers have come up with designs which allow for microphones to have other pickup patterns than their natural one, or even better, microphones which possess multiple switchable patterns!

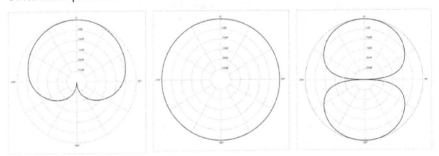

Figure 6 Microphone Pickup Patterns[4] The line delimits the area in which the microphone picks up sound the best, usually at 1 kHz

---

[4] From [7], reproduced with permission under the GNU Free Documentation License; credit to Galak76

Sound pickup patterns can be engineered by multiple means, including multiple capsule designs and phase shifting (or delaying) the sound coming from certain angles.

Pickup patterns are usually represented in the form of a polar diagram, representing its sensitivity from all angles around the capsule, from maximum pickup (0 dB) on the outside and less pickup on the inside of the diagram.

What do the different patterns do?

The first is called *cardioid* (C) and picks up sound better from the front of the microphone (usually indicated by a small sign on the front of the microphone; here, the front of the microphone is the top of the picture). The second is called *omnidirectional* (O) and picks up sound equally well from all directions. The third is called *figure 8* (8) and picks up sound well from the front and rear. One pattern not depicted here is the super cardioid pattern (SC): its shape is the same as the cardioid but the microphone picks up less sound from the sides (90° and 270° angles in Figure 6).

Pickup patterns depend on the frequency; for example, lower frequencies tend to be picked up from all angles well, no matter what the intended pickup pattern is, because they are less sensitive to obstacles (like a diaphragm) than higher frequencies; also, the method used to construct the pickup pattern might not treat all frequencies equally; those are the reasons why manufacturers might display more than one frequency on their microphone polar pattern plots. If they do not, the pickup pattern shown will be at 1 kHz.

Why do I need different patterns?

Pickup patterns are important in audio recording because choosing the right pattern can make mixing much easier later. For example, if you want to precisely record a snare drum without picking up too much of the cymbal, you will choose a directional microphone, pointing its area of best sensitivity towards the snare – and its blind side towards the cymbal to minimize the spill of sound from the cymbal into the microphone (this is called *bleed*). If you are recording a classical orchestra, you might want a microphone which picks up sound from all directions to capture the ensemble rather than some instruments.

I want to buy a microphone, help me!

Next is a table giving you a summary of the best microphones in the business, some old, some more recent. Most of these names are known in audio circles; they are usually known for use in certain situations. A "+" sign in the pattern column means that other patterns are available for the microphone, usually through a switch on the front or detachable microphone heads.

Manufacturer	Model	Type	Price	Pattern	Famous for
AKG	C414	LDC	$1000	C, O, 8, +	Instruments, drums
AKG	C451	Condenser[5]	$350	C, O, 8, +	Drum overheads
AKG	D112	Dynamic	$120	C	Kick drum
Audio-Technica	AT4033[6]	LDC	$350	C	Bass, kick drum
Cascade	FAT HEAD	Ribbon	$175	8	Brass
Electro-Voice	RE20	Dynamic	$400	C	Lush instruments
Neumann	KM84	SDC	$1100	C	Strings
Neumann	U47 FET	LDC	$4000	SC	Kick, bass, male vocals
Neumann	U67	LDC	--	C, O, 8	Vocals, overheads
Rode	NT-1A	LDC	$250	C	Tight budgets
Royer	R-121	Ribbon	$1295	8	Loud instrum., rooms
Sennheiser	MD421 II	Dynamic	$350	C	Drum toms
Shure	SM57	Dynamic	$100	C	Guitar cabinets, vocals
Shure	SM7B	Dynamic	$350	C	Vocals
Sony	C-37A	LDC	--	C, O	Everything
Studio Projects	C1	LDC	$250	C	Tight budgets

Table 4 Characteristics of Some Known Microphones

In this book, prices are mentioned to give you an idea of the required investment to acquire the item; you can find it used for cheaper – or not at all; I have noticed a general 10% per year price drop for most audio equipment, with some exceptions: some devices have gone up in price in recent years.

---

[5] Size of diaphragm unknown
[6] The AT4050 is the same microphone with two more pickup patterns: figure 8 and omnidirectional

You will sometimes see a microphone dubbed as another older microphone's "successor". What manufacturers mean is that they intend to produce microphones with the same revered characteristics as their ancestors; unfortunately, these newer models are not always faithful descendants, so make sure to read up on them before thinking you just made a great deal. I will also mention copies which look the same from the outside but are very different on the inside.

Microphone Placement

Finding a good sounding spot and placing a well-chosen microphone there will go a long way in giving you a good sound to work with later: "get it right at the source", instead of trying to "fix it in the mix".

Why do I care about microphone placement?

Microphone placement is the secret sauce that many recording engineers use to get their sound. There are no general rules, but the closer to the source the microphone is, the less natural it will sound and the more processing it will need – this is sometimes desirable (e.g. guitar cabinet). Also, when a microphone is placed close to the sound source, it risks favoring picking up low frequencies, an effect called *proximity effect*. Moving the microphone further out from the source gives a more natural (reverberant) sound, but if the recording space is not acoustically treated, those sound reverberations will influence the recorded sound in a negative manner (see Section 4.3). Sometimes, placement distance to the source is not an option because of bleed issues; in those cases, angling the microphone in different ways helps getting a better sound. The best way to find your sound is to start from what the pros do and move on from there. After a while, you will have your own set of microphone placements.

2.3. A Note on Impedance

Once converted into voltage by the microphone capsule, our sound enters the electrical realm[7]. We have talked about voltages so far because that is what is physically changed in the processes we described; however, when those voltages are transmitted along conductors like cables, it is more convenient to discuss about currents; both are linked by resistance or impedance.

---

[7] For a really clear explanation of how electronics work, see [8]

What is impedance?

There, components transmitting the current, like cables, can alter it. They have electrical characteristics like resistance, which has some resemblance to friction in the mechanical world. Because currents transmitted by audio equipment vary with time (alternating currents are either generated or modulated by transducers), the correct concept to use is *impedance* instead of resistance[8].

Why? According to the laws of physics, two phenomena appear when tensions (or currents) change with time: a magnetic field appears (*induction effect*) and electrical charge is stored in the conductor (*capacitance effect*), both increasing the factors impeding (hence the term "impedance") the current from flowing to its destination: inductive reactance X_L (from the induction effect) and capacitive reactance X_C (from the capacitance effect) form the *reactance* X:

$$X = X_L + X_C$$

Equation 4 Reactance

with $X_L = 2\,\pi * v * L$ and $X_C = \frac{1}{2\,\pi * v * C}$.

L is the inductance (measured in Henrys) of the material used and C is its capacitance (measured in Farads). Note that inductive reactance is proportional to the audio frequency v while capacitive reactance is inversely proportional to it: this means that at low frequencies, inductive reactance is small but capacitive reactance is large, the opposite being true at high frequencies. Impedance is simply the sum of those two effects, resistance and reactance. The symbol for impedance is Z and it is measured in Ohms (Ω), like resistance:

$$Z = \sqrt{R^2 + X^2}$$

Equation 5 Impedance

where R is the resistance, X is the *reactance*. That is where the "Z" on your audio interface comes from.

---

[8] See [9] for a complete discussion of the concept

HiZ, LowZ: what is that about?

Because different devices translate pressure into electricity (like microphones) or transport electricity (like cables) in different ways by design, they have different impedances and, thus, transport current with varying friction. There generally are two types of impedances related to audio equipment: high impedance (usually labelled HiZ) and low impedance (usually labelled LowZ). Low impedance devices (0-10kΩ, 1 kΩ = 1000 Ω) include most microphones, interface inputs for microphones and most interface outputs. For example, my interface has three types of input impedances: microphone at 2400 Ω, mic/line at 10kΩ and guitar at 1 MΩ; the output is at 100 Ω. High impedance devices (> 10 kΩ) include instrument outputs (generally between 7 and 20 kΩ) and interface instrument inputs (in the 1 MΩ range).

Why is impedance important?

Because in some situations, knowing the source and destination device impedances (destination impedance can also be called the *load*) can help resolve audio issues like loss of sound quality. Most of the time, impedance issues are transparent because of the way audio equipment is built: to ensure a problem-less signal transmission, the target impedance is at least 10 times that of the source. This ensures that voltages are properly transferred across multiple devices so that the signal quality is preserved.

2.4. Cables

Why do I care about cables?

Connecting the microphone to whatever comes next in the signal chain is an *audio cable*. An audio cable is made of conducting material surrounded by shielding material. Its role at this stage is to carry the electrical current generated by the microphone to the preamp. Because electrical current is subject to interferences by other electrical devices or magnetic devices, and because one can generate the other, shielding is needed so that the electrical current (carrying all the information of the recorded sound!) can arrive at its destination safe and sound.

Cable impedance effects are generally negligible because they come into effect only when the highest frequency present in the signal corresponds to about 10 times the cable length. For example, a 20 kHz frequency is equivalent to a wavelength of about 10 km: Equation 2 applies, but here, speed is the speed of light, that is the speed at which electromagnetic waves travel through the medium; because there is resistance (impedance) to the progression of those waves in a cable, the waves do not travel at the full speed of light of around 300'000'000 m/s but at a fraction of its speed: that fraction is called the *velocity factor VF* and it depends, without any surprise, on the capacitance C and the inductance L of the material used for the cable.

Balanced and unbalanced cables: what are they?

There are two types of cables: *unbalanced* and *balanced*. Unbalanced cables use only two conductors: a central conductor, carrying the changing current, and a shield connected to ground. Examples of unbalanced cables are ¼ inch guitar cables or older RCA connectors. Balanced cables use three conductors, two in the middle to carry the changing current, and the last one for shielding purposes.

The advantage of balanced cables is that because there are two conductors, they can be designed so that interferences cancel out. Examples of balanced cables are XLR connectors and TRS connectors. While TRS does stand for *Tip Ring Sleeve*, XLR does not stand for Ground (X) Left Right as many people think it does[9].

Most images found on the web being legally protected against copying, simply type "balanced unbalanced connectors" into any search engine, select "Images" et voilà: all sorts of nicely drawn connectors, from RCA to TS to TRS to XLR.

It is important to know the difference because unbalanced cables should only be connected to other unbalanced cables to avoid ground loop issues. Cables can be recognized by their type to be balanced or unbalanced (see above); in case of doubt, device manufacturers usually indicate which type of connector you are dealing with.

To read a more detailed discussion of cables, please see [3]; balanced and unbalanced cables are discussed in [11].

---

[9] For the truth, read [10]: it has to do with how cables were once built

2.5. Microphone Preamplifiers

What is a microphone preamplifier?

When the sound has been captured by the microphone (we should say "read by the microphone), it comes out in the form of electrical current tension values. Those values are usually very small since the air pressure moving the membrane is not very strong: on average, 0.1 mV for a ribbon microphone and 10 mV for a dynamic microphone; guitar pickup levels are higher at 150-200 mV[10].

Audio equipment is designed to work with much higher voltages (around 1V, the line level we previously defined), so this electrical current must be amplified. That is the role of preamplifiers, or *preamps* or *pres* (pronounced "preez"): help the signal *gain* power. How these devices amplify the signal is important since we know that any electronic component put in the electrical flow will alter the original signal[11].

How does a preamp work?

A preamp consists in a chain of electronic components. First, the input, usually a (balanced) male XLR input since that is what microphones usually use as outputs. The next set of components can be put under the banner of the *input section* and is optional, depending on the preamp model; some have these components (and more), and some have none. The first component in the input is usually a phantom power source for condenser microphones. The next component might be a polarity switch which would allow you to flip the polarity of the incoming signal. Then, a pad switch might allow you to make the source quieter if it is too loud by inserting a set of coupled resistances in series in the circuit. Finally, a resistance inserted in parallel with the circuit might be available to change the impedance of the circuit; the switch itself might be labeled "Low Z", for example.

Once these formalities have been executed, the real deal starts with the main gain stage and the actual increase in tension for which the preamp is built. This increase is achieved by inserting in the circuit a series of electronic components such as transistors, vacuum tubes, operational amplifiers (op-amps) and/or a combination of all the above, each raising the gain by some fixed amount called *gain stage*.

---

[10] See [3] for details
[11] For a detailed discussion, see [12] and [13]

These components can change the way the signal is shaped and add frequencies that the original signal did not have: that is where the secret sauce of mic pres is made and a jealously kept secret. If those effects are not desired (a so-called *clean signal* is preferred), a copy of the original signal is inserted after the gain stage and mixed with the processed signal to try and get rid of the unwanted effect(s); this works because the gain stage flips the polarity of the signal[12]. Finally, the output buffer takes the amplified signal and feeds it to the next device in the signal chain. Other components such as a trim switch might help you adapt the pre's output to the next device input sensitivity.

One such line of components, built to amplify an analog signal, is called a *channel*. You will hear engineers talk about "4 channels of input": this means that they can record four analog sources and amplifies those signals simultaneously.

How do we categorize preamps?

Preamps can be classified in multiple fashions, but the most useful one is the one which categorizes them by what type of amplifiers are used for the main gain stage: solid-state or tube. Solid-state devices are devices which have current flow only through solid matter, by opposition to tube devices which have current go through vacuum tubes. Solid-state amplifiers include all types of transistors, bipolar junction transistors, field-effect transistors, and op-amps; these transistors can be put on integrated circuits (IC) or separately integrated in the signal flow (the famous *discrete design* which minimizes interferences between signals in the device itself). There are preamps which gain stage the signal through a solid-state amplifier before sending it through a tube; technically speaking, they are a solid-state preamp.

On the topic of tube vs. solid-state amplifiers and which ones sound the best, we are touching upon religion, much like in the analog vs. digital debate. The only sensible thing which can be said is that people favor the tube / analog sound because those designs produce mostly even harmonics which are musical to our ears (the famous warmth that people talk about). Tube amps are usually both noisier and less accurate than solid-state amps, but we have learned to like the "old" sound better and that is what we now expect. I strongly believe that if we were to present

---

[12] That is how transistors work, see [8] for more details

both amplified sounds next to the source to a Martian audiophile, our Martian friend would prefer the solid-state / digital sound for its better accuracy.

I want to buy a preamp, help me!

In the table below, classic preamps are listed. They are chosen because they were made from respected and well-known manufacturers. The features column contains the number of channels ("c"), the type of electronics inside ("SS" for solid-state and "T" for tube) and the design (see below). The last column gives an indication on how most people perceive the sound coming out of the preamp – do not quote me on that!

Manufacturer	Model	Features	Price	Per channel	Sound
A Designs	Pacifica	2c, SS, A	$2100	$1050	Thick
API	3124+	4c, SS, AB	$2800	$700	
Avalon	AD2022	2c, SS, A	$3000	$1500	
BAE Audio	1073MP	1c, SS, A	$1000	$1000	Neve 1073 clone
FMR Audio	RNP 8380	2c, SS, A	$450	$225	Clean
Focusrite	ISA One	1c, SS	$500	$500	"Colored"
George Massenburg Labs	GML 8304	4c, SS, A	$3600	$900	Clean
Golden Age	Pre73 MK II	1c, SS, A	$350	$350	Neve 1073 clone
Grace Design	m101	1c, SS	$765	$765	Clean
Great River	MP-2NV	2c, SS, A	$2275	$1138	Neve 1073 clone
Neve	1073	1c, SS, A	--	--	Big, punchy
Telefunken	V72	1c, T, A	$1300	$1300	Thick
True Systems	P-Solo	1c, SS	$600	$600	"Colored"
Universal Audio	LA-610 MKII	1c, T	$1600	$1600	Warm

Table 5 Characteristics of Some Known Preamps

Another classification considers the design of the internals of the preamp. There are three main designs: *Class A, Class B* and *Class AB*. Class A designs signal the fact that both the positive and negative voltages are simultaneously amplified. This means that the output signal's shape is very close to the original (no distortion), but also that the device will run very hot since it is functioning all the time; this means more risk of failure. Class B solves this problem by having two distinct amplifiers, one to amplify the positive and one the negative voltages; the disadvantage is that at the crossover between both sides, the signal may be distorted because the amplifying devices take some small time to start working; thus, they are perceived to be less accurate than their Class A counterparts. The third type, Class AB, tries to take the best of both worlds by having the following amplifier starting up before the crossover is reached so that when it does, the distortion is minimized. As you can see, Class A does not mean that it is the best class, only that it is one design amongst others.

Manufacturers have been very creative in bundling different devices together in a single cased product, appearing as a single device to the unsuspecting consumer. Such bundles include the *audio interface*, which consists in one or more mic preamps, along with AD and DA converters. Another bundle is the *channel strip*, putting together mic preamps and outboard gear (see Section 2.7) such as EQ (EQ stands for *equalizer*) and compressors.

To close this short summary of how preamps work, I have always wondered what the difference was between, on one hand, turning the knob on the preamp clockwise, and on the other, turning the knob on my speakers clockwise. To me, both knob turning exercises achieved the same goal: making the music louder. As it turns out, the difference is significant: the knob on the preamp amplifies the signal before processing: it gives the processors down the chain more "meat" to work with. The knob on the speaker only amplifies the signal after processing.

2.6. Effects

What are effects: how do they help me?
We now know that an audio signal has three characteristics: intensity (or volume), frequency and phase (see Equation 2). Each characteristic can be modified by cleverly placing electronic components in the sound's signal path. In Table 6, basic processor or *effect units* (or *effects*, or, for even lazier people, *FX*) are displayed.

Let us study this table for a bit. First, you will notice that there are three main types of effects: those who work with intensity (or volume, also called *dynamics processors*), those who work in the frequency domain and those who work in the time domain. Technically speaking, the phaser obviously works with phase, but since it works with phase with respect to time, it is always put in the time domain processor category. Tremolo is an effect which modulates the volume of the original signal; it is in this sense an offshoot of both the compressor (modulating down) and the expander (modulating up).

Effect	Type	Result	Derived effects
Gate	Intensity	Cleaner sound	
Compressor	Intensity	Cleaner sound Colored sound	Limiter Transient shaper
Expander	Intensity	Cleaner sound Colored sound	Tremolo
Distortion	Frequency	Colored sound	
Equalizer	Frequency	Cleaner sound Colored sound	Vocoder, wah-wah
Phaser	Time	Colored sound	
Delay	Time	Colored sound	Reverb, flanger, chorus

Table 6 Effects

It might look like a theoretical separation, but knowing what you are working on can help you troubleshoot what the effect is doing when the results do not sound good; furthermore, generally speaking, clean-up effects should always be used before coloring effects for a very simple reason: you do not want to be coloring or enhancing parts of the sound that you do not like. Second, what you obtain when passing a signal through one of these effects (the results column) can be sorted out in two categories: a cleaner sound or a colored sound. A cleaner sound means that the effect has been used to remove some undesirable feature of the sound.

For example, a *gate* might be used to clean up background noise; a *compressor* might be used to even out a performance; an *expander* might be used to bring up an interviewee's speech level to the interviewer's for a better listening experience; an *EQ* might be used to remove some low frequency build-up from a bass amp or an offending frequency caused by a cheap microphone. In all the examples above, the result is a sound cleaned up and prepared either for further processing (most likely) or for direct listening.

What does coloring sound mean?
The phrase "colored sound" might sound weird: how can a sound be colored? What most people mean by that is how their perception of the sound has been altered, usually in a pleasing way.

For example, you have seen some preamps labeled as delivering a "colored" sound in Table 5: the preamp adds frequency content (the "color") by amplifying the signal through certain electronic components. In the case of effects, the same principle applies. A compressor might color a snare drum sound by letting the initial hit sound go through but reducing the volume afterwards to "tighten up" the sound; a transient shaper might make a cymbal hit sound for longer by increasing the duration of the sound; a tremolo might give a guitar sound this old groovy 60s sound by rapidly varying its volume (not its frequency!); no need to explain how the distortion changes the sound, you rarely hear a non-distorted electric guitar these days; an EQ might color the sound by adding high frequencies to an otherwise dull flute solo; a Vocoder might restrict the frequency range of a vocal performance, giving it the famous robotic feel; a Wah-wah pedal might make a guitar solo much funkier by modulating the original notes with a sweep of some frequency range (think Jimi Hendrix); a flanger or a chorus might make a guitar sound much weirder by changing its phase and remixing the processed signal with the original (think The Police); a delay or reverb might make a sound seem bigger by playing copies of the original signal right after the original, emulating reflections from surrounding walls (think Pink Floyd, or any progressive rock band for that matter). Of course, these effects can be chained one after the other, making creativity with even a simple original sound infinite.

The original signal can be modified with those effects by two different means, or, more precisely, in two different domains. Because we are still in the analog domain (our signal still has not been converted to digital bits), those effects would logically be produced by hardware units which include tubes, filters, transformers, etc. Some of these units have become famous and will be mentioned in Section 2.7. In the digital age, some of these units' effects have been modelled in software called *plugins*. Some of these plugins will be mentioned in Section 3.3.

These effects usually share one characteristic: the original (*dry*) sound can be mixed with the processed (*wet*) sound to change the amount of effect added to or subtracted from the signal. If the device does not possess this feature, splitting the signal to two tracks at mixing stage and varying the relative volume of both tracks yields the same result. Also, each of these effects can be used to trigger other effects, yet increasing the complexity of what can be achieved with just a handful of processors.

Let us now dive into what each effect does and what its main parameters are.

Intensity Effects

Gate

What is a gate?

A *gate* allows a signal to pass only if it is below a certain *threshold*. This can be used in various situations: to clean up unwanted noise from a recording, or to filter a signal to then pass on the "on/off" information to another signal for further processing (this is called *triggering*).

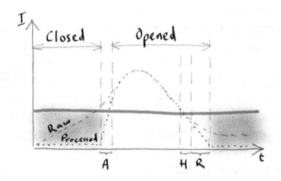

Figure 7 Gate Parameters *The graph displays the signal intensity with respect to time; the raw signal is the dashed line; the processed signal is the dotted line; the intensity threshold is the thick horizontal line; A stands for Attack time, H for Hold time, R for Release time.*

In Figure 7, you can see an incoming raw signal increasing in intensity; a noise gate is placed on its path. When the signal's intensity crosses the threshold, the gates starts to open and the processed signal appears; it finishes opening when the *attack* time has passed. At the end of the attack time, the unprocessed and processed signals are the same. When the incoming signal's intensity gets smaller than the threshold, the gate is programmed to wait a set amount of time (the *hold* time) before it starts shutting down; during the hold time, the unprocessed and processed signals are still the same. When the hold time is over, the gate starts to shut down and the processed signal's intensity decreases; the gate finishes to shut down when the *release* time has passed; when the gate is closed, the processed signal disappears. You could also set the gate to reduce the signal's intensity by some fixed amount – the *range*. In the example, the gate's range is infinite: this means that when the gate is closed, the processed signal's intensity is zero.

How do you reduce a signal's intensity?

That is where *Digital Signal Processing* comes in; it is an engineering discipline that studies how signals are measured and transformed. In a nutshell, reducing a signal's intensity is achieved in the physical world simply by placing electronic components (filters) in its path; circuit design determines the type of filtering. In the plugins effect world, programming models the behavior of those components[13].

When do I use a gate?

A first example of gate use would be when you are trying to take out room noise from a live recording: set the threshold right above the noise maximum level and only the louder parts of the signal will go through. You could of course manually lower the volume of the signal every time nothing useful is being recorded, but that would be tedious and open to a lot of mistakes; recording these knob movements (here: the intensity of the signal) to replay them is called *automation*.

A second example of gate use would be if you would like to trigger an echo whenever the vocals go above a certain loudness: you would set up the threshold high so that only the loudest parts of the vocals would be let through by the gate and then use that information to trigger the echo; this process is called *side-chaining*: using the information from one signal to trigger changes on another signal.

Compressors

What is a compressor?

Air is a natural compressor, so our ears are used to listening to a compressed sound: that is why the compressor is one of the most used effect in the industry, trying the recreate the sensation of listening to live sound. A *compressor* effectively smoothes out signal peaks to a more uniform signal. You can use this effect, for example, to catch unwanted peaks in a vocal or a guitar recording; you could also use it to bring more coherence to an overall recording by limiting the difference between its

---

[13] For an excellent overview of Digital Signal Processing, please see [14]

quietest and loudest parts. Another way of saying the same thing is: a compressor limits the *dynamic range* of a signal[14].

What does "dynamic range" mean?

It is the ratio of the loudest possible intensity (volume) to the *noise floor*, defined as the quietest possible intensity of the signal. By now, when you hear "ratio", you think dB. We saw that a typical dynamic microphone outputs voltages in the 10-mV region, and that a typical processing device works with voltages in the 1V range; from Equation 3, we know that the ratio of amplitudes x is expressed in dB with $20\ log_{10}\ x$ so in our case, the ratio is 40 dB – that is the gain needed from the microphone preamp but also the dynamic range available to the engineer recording the sound.

How does a compressor work?

A standard compressor has three main components: a level detector, a gain reduction module and an output amplifier. The level detector's jobs are, 1) to see when the incoming signal's intensity is above a set *threshold*, 2) how fast it has to start sending the reduction information to the gain reduction module (*attack* "time"), and 3): how fast it has to stop sending it (*release* "time"). Yes, you read that right: the attack and release « times » are speeds; depending on manufacturers or developers, the compressor filters are even specified differently for attack and release. For example, attack filters are usually specified in the amount of time it takes for a set percentage of the gain reduction target to be achieved, which means settling for less; that percentage ranges from 70-95%. Release filters are usually specified in the amount of time it takes for a 10-dB gain reduction to happen.

The gain reduction module's job is to aim at reducing the signal's intensity by using a series of filters; the compression goal is called a *compression ratio*. You notice that I do not say "compresses" but "aims at reducing"; it is not to be pedantic: compressors do not simply reduce intensity, they reduce intensity by comparing the current intensity with the previous intensity because that is how filters work; this means you cannot just "tell the signal to stick below a certain threshold".

The output amplifier's job is to increase the signal's intensity by an amount called the *makeup gain* so that the sound has the same intensity it had

---

[14] For a nice detailed discussion, see [3] and the corresponding Wikipedia article

before entering the compressor. The gain can be reduced right when the information is received by the level detector (*hard knee*); alternatively, it can be smoothed out by using a smaller ratio before using the full desired ratio on the signal (*soft knee*).

You might hear some people say that a compressor brings quiet parts of the signal up. That is not true of a compressor as a part of its standard operation: it merely aims at shaving off peaks going above the threshold. Only if you make up for the lost gain by increasing the processed signal's output will the quiet parts of the processed signal be heard more: that is what the makeup gain is for.

In the list of effects shown in Table 6, the compressor is the first major effect that you will be hearing a lot about in audio circles and online forums. One of the reasons is because it is very widely used, but I believe that it is also talked about with a shroud of mystery because it is very rarely completely understood – let us hope that what you just read put you on the right track.

Limiter

A *limiter* is a compressor with a very large ratio. This is of course theoretical in the analog domain, as the components used limit what the limiter can achieve.

Transient Shaper

What is a transient?

Transient is an adjective meaning "passing especially quickly into and out of existence" (from the Merriam Webster dictionary); in the audio world, a transient (noun) is that concept applied to a signal or sound. A lot of people talk about transients and mean the percussive element or the initial attack of a sound, like a snare drum hit or a strung guitar string; other people mean the shape of the waveform, and that is what a transient shaper refers to: shaping the waveform of a sound.

How does a transient shaper work?

A *transient shaper* has only two parameters, which makes it simple to use but very powerful at the same time. The first parameter allows increasing or decreasing the gain on the attack of the transient; the corresponding knob is usually labeled *attack*. You might think that this is exactly what a compressor with make-up gain does; you would be right, except that there is a difference: the compressor only works above a certain threshold while the transient shaper diligently increases or decreases the gain on every voltage it sees. The second parameter, linked to the first, allows increasing or decreasing the gain on the tail end of a waveform; this button is usually labeled *sustain* or *release*. There usually also is a *gain* button to control the output of the effect.

Learning how to properly use a transient shaper can be a great help when a compressor does not work or an EQ is too blunt of a tool. I would even recommend using a transient shaper before starting to use a compressor simply because it is much more intuitive and easy to understand. I know their uses are different, but there are times when increasing the gain on a transient is better than trying to make the transient coming out by reducing the dynamic range of the signal. If the compressor is the well-known superhero (think Iron Man), the transient shaper is the unsung superhero who comes out of nowhere to save your day when you think all has been lost (think Gollum).

Expander

An *expander*, sometimes also called an upward compressor, is the exact opposite of a compressor (or downward compressor): it increases the dynamic range of a signal. In this regard, it is a type of gate: it can make quiet signals even quieter by comparison to louder parts by increasing the dynamic range of a signal. Expanders are not the most talked-about effects but are worth knowing about.

Frequency Effects

Distortion

What is distortion?
Distortion is an effect which is caused by inserting electronic devices in the signal path to limit or clip the original voltage signal. In audio terms, the result is that frequencies that were not present in the original signal appear in the processed signal. Odd or even harmonics appear in *harmonic distortion*, while combinations of the original frequencies appear in *intermodulation distortion*. The first type will always sound "musical" since multiples of the original frequencies are, for each frequency, simply octaves above the original. For intermodulation distortion, this might not be the case

since a sum or difference in two frequencies might not yield a frequency related to the original frequency[15].

Depending on the type of overtone added by the electronic circuit, the resulting signal will have a different shape. For example, adding an odd harmonic to the original signal will approximate a square wave, while adding an even harmonic will approximate a saw-tooth wave. Combining these will affect and change the original signal in different ways[16].

Is distortion, fuzz and overdrive the same?

The guitarists among you will want to know the difference between distortion, overdrive and fuzz: are they the same? No, they are not. Overdrive is exactly what the name indicates: pushing (driving) the amplifier into generating harmonics by pushing the electronics in the amp past their intended power range; this means that in overdrive, the main goal is to gain power, with adding color a secondary objective; thus, the processed sound is different from the original, but not by much. Distortion is the opposite: the goal is to mess with the original signal as much as possible, with some power gain along the way. Fuzz is obtained by inserting special transistors in the signal path which add frequencies to the sound, recognizable by its warm and "fuzzy" character (think Jimi Hendrix).

In our effect terminology, distortion (meant in the generic sense) is clearly a coloring tool. All sorts of different devices and tricks can be used to distort the original signal: permanently damaging amplifiers, using devices in unintended ways, etc. In the digital domain, people spend fortunes on software to try and reproduce those analog "warm-sounding" distortion effects.

Equalizer

What is an equalizer?

An *equalizer* (*EQ*) effect modifies the gain on certain frequencies, either down (*cut*) or up (*boost*). It is a very well-known feature of many HiFi home stereo systems. It might be popular because turning nobs has a direct impact on the outgoing sound and a repeatable impact at that. The same

---

[15] See [3] for more details on distortion
[16] See [15] for a very nice graphical description of the distortion effect

applies to audio: the equalizer is the most famous effect in the audio engineer's bag of tricks.

EQ effects can be simply specified with three parameters describing how the signal responds to the components placed in its path: the shape of the EQ change, the frequency at which the equalization happens and the speed with which the effect comes into play.

What are pass, shelf and band filters?

EQ shapes come in three kinds: pass, shelf, and band. A *pass filter* lets every frequency above (high) or below (low) through. Another (opposite) way of thinking about it is to talk about cut instead of pass: low cut is high pass and high cut is low pass; I will stick to pass because I think it is more intuitive.

In Figure 8, we see a *high pass filter*: the high-pass frequency is defined as the frequency which falls below the original frequency by 3 dB. The speed (or the slope) with which the EQ change happens is usually expressed in dB per octave or dB/oct. Specifying this type of EQ would then mean saying that it is a 300 Hz high-pass filter at -12 dB/oct. Remember that an octave is the frequency distance between two equivalent notes, e.g. C3 – C4, so, yes, this means that -12 dB/oct is not the same intensity reduction at 100 Hz than at 10kHz.

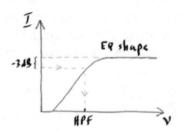

Figure 8 High Pass Filter *The graph displays the signal intensity with respect to frequency; HPF stands for High Pass Frequency.*

A *shelf filter* is the combination of a pass and an inverted pass filter around a specific frequency. In Figure 9, we see a shelf filter consisting in high pass filters (dotted line) with a cut in low frequencies and a boost in high frequencies, and a shelf filter consisting in low pass filters (full line) with a boost in low frequencies and a cut in high frequencies. Exactly like for the pass filter, the slope in dB/octave determines how quickly the changes happen.

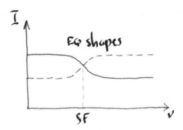

Figure 9 Shelf EQ *The graph displays the signal intensity with respect to frequency for two filters: high pass (dotted line) and low pass (full line); SF stands for Shelf Frequency.*

What is a first order filter?

Both filters are obtained with what are called first order filters: in the analog world, that is what the combination of a single resistor and a single capacitor can produce. Because of their simple design, these filters can only produce those filter shapes depicted above. For more complex filters like the *band pass filters*, which lets frequencies within a range pass (you could describe it like a combination of a high and low pass filter), we need to go to so-called second-order filters because of the mathematical functions involved in describing the frequency response to the filter. Here, an extra parameter applies: Q ; it tells us how wide the frequency change is:

$$Q = \frac{v_0}{v_R - v_L}$$

Equation 6 EQ Q

where v_0 is the center frequency, v_R is the right frequency when the EQ curve is -3 dB from its highest point and v_L is the left frequency when the EQ curve is +3 dB from its highest point. A high Q means that the EQ change will happen over a very narrow bandwidth.

How do I use an equalizer?

Taking frequencies out of the signal is usually associated with cleaning up the sound (for example, taking low frequency rumble off a bass guitar recording). Of course, cleaning up in this fashion also colors the sound in some way – after all, we are changing how the sound sounds; however, I will stick to thinking about EQ cuts as cleaning because that is the easiest way to think about it. Cuts are generally made with a small Q (narrow width); this sounds more musical to a lot of professionals, but as always with audio, feel free to experiment. Adding frequencies is usually done with a larger Q (wider width); again, experimenting is the key, but starting off with a larger Q will help you keep your track sounding musical.

EQ cuts should be made before applying any other effects, especially compression, while EQ boosts should be made later. The reason is that compression will bring out the quieter more subdued parts of the sound, like breaths, or string noises. If you do not remove these parasites, for example with EQ cuts, they will appear to be louder in the compressed sound. EQ boosts, on the other hand, will stand out more if applied after compression, even if in theory, you could apply them before compression as well; in that case, keep the boost small and wide, otherwise compression will make the change even more dramatic.

I will mention one trick you can use to find out offending frequencies. First, listen to the sound and try to determine where the issue is frequency-wise. Once you have the frequency range in mind, apply EQ to the track with a very narrow Q and a very large gain boost and sweep the frequency range, going back and forth a few times; once you have spotted the offending frequency, simply reverse the gain from a large boost to a large cut.

Vocoder

A *vocoder* is an EQ filter applied to a vocal track; it is a good example of a coloring effect using EQ cuts. Different settings can be used, but good starting points are a lower bound of 500 Hz and an upper bound of 3400 Hz.

Wah-wah

The *wah-wah* effect is an EQ filter which periodically in time adds and subtracts high frequencies to and from a sound. The effect name does in fact represent the effect itself: the "a" vowel represents the sound with added frequencies while the "w" represents the sound with subtracted frequencies.

Time Effects

Phaser

What is a phaser?

A *phaser* or phasor is an effect that creates cuts and boosts in the sound's frequencies by altering the sound's phase over time. The way this is achieved is by placing an all-pass filter in the signal path: all frequencies go through but the phase relationship between them is changed by varying the phase with respect to frequency. All filters alter the signal's phase because their impedance "delay" it.

How does a phaser work?

This is how it works: the incoming signal is split in two; the first signal has its phase altered as described above; it is then mixed back into the second (original) signal; what happens then is that the out-of-phase signal frequencies cancel out while the in-phase signal frequencies are boosted. The peaks thus created are unevenly spaced; this means that they are not in a harmonic (multiple) relationship with the original frequencies. This gives the characteristic "eeeaaaaaooooaaaaaeeee" effect known mostly as a guitar effect, but also worthwhile as a keyboard effect.

Figure 10 Phaser The incoming signal goes through the splitter (S); one version of the signal goes through a phase change before being recombined in the mixer (M) with the original signal.

Phasers might have different parameters depending on how they are built, but they have at least a frequency to determine how quickly the phase is changed, a range of swept frequencies and a feedback control to determine how much (if any) of the signal processed should be fed back into the original unprocessed signal. Feeding the signal back into the input is a way to increase the magnitude of the effect. Van Halen is known for its uses of phasers, especially in "Atomic Punk" (jump to 0:50), but other bands such as Queen, Genesis (on keyboards) and Radiohead also used it.

Delay

What is a delay?

A *delay* mixes a delayed version of a signal with itself. The result is a single echo or a series of echoes, depending on how many times the sound is split and fed back (delayed) into itself.

How does a delay work?

A delay effect essentially has one parameter: the amount of time the signal should be delayed by; this amount of time can be expressed in ms or in relationship to the song rhythm, e.g. in 1/8 note increments; the latter can help keep the delay "musical", meant as in "with some level of coherence with the song". A feedback control might also be present like for the phaser. Because of the apparent space gained by delaying a signal by small amounts, delay effects are sometimes used to create fake stereo images from a mono signal; the danger of that technique is that when the song is listened in mono, the combing effect resulting from the addition of two delayed signals will produce a flanging effect (see below).

Figure 11 Delay *The incoming signal goes through the splitter (S); one version of the signal is delayed before being recombined in the mixer (M) with the original signal.*

A delay effect can be hard to spot because very short delays (15-60ms depending on the relative delay level) fall below our conscious listening threshold. The larger the delay is, the quieter the delayed copy can be before the effect is detected. When the delay is increased beyond our hearing threshold, it first gives a sense of spaciousness, even if our brain does not recognize both signals as being distinct. If it is increased further, the delayed signal is perceived as a distinct echo of the original sound. Delay effects are used by a lot of guitarists to thicken their sound, but perhaps the most well-known user of delay is The Edge from U2 (check out the intro to "Where the Streets Have No Name" or "One Tree Hill").

Reverb

What is reverb?

A *reverb* effect is a more complex version of a delay: it mimics the reverberation (hence the name) or reflections of a sound in a confined space. Each time the original sound bounces off a reflecting surface, it creates an echo (a delayed copy of itself for a certain listening position inside the space) which decays over time depending on the sound's frequency and conditions inside the space. Reverb is what you hear when you place a source in a room, play it and then abruptly stop it. Those multiple slightly altered less powerful versions of the source sound are interpreted by our brains as an indication that the source was played in a space.

What is RT_{60}?

The time it takes for the sound to die off is called RT_{60} for *Reverberation Time*; it is the time it takes for the signal to decay by 60 dB; RT_{60} depends on the volume of the space V and on the inverse of both the total surface area of the room S and the absorption coefficient a of the material used to define the space (valid at 20 degrees Celsius or 68 degrees Fahrenheit):

$$RT_{60} \sim 0.16 * \frac{V}{S * a}$$

Equation 7 RT60

It also depends on the frequency of the sound through the absorption coefficient. In a typical room of 4 meters by 3 meters by 2.4 meters (roughly 13 feet by 10 feet by 8 feet for you Imperials out there), $RT_{60} \sim \frac{0.08}{a}$. For plaster walls[17], a is about 0.02, so RT_{60} is 4 seconds! Make your walls hardwood ($a \sim 0.3$) and the time falls to 0.267 seconds or 267 milliseconds. I am not going to make this an acoustics discussion, but the way your recording and mixing space is built (and treated, if necessary) is much more important than the gear you will buy[18].

---

[17] See [16]
[18] This is discussed in details on the interwebz; for a start, check out [17]

What are the different types of reverbs?

The first analog reverb effect is to simply play a prerecorded sound in a room and have a microphone pick up the resulting sound- this is called a *chamber reverb*.

The second type of analog reverb is the *plate reverb*: sound is sent through a speaker-like device to the center of a thin metal sheet suspended in a sound-proofed box; pickups are mounted on the plate to detect vibrations induced by the transmitted sound; those vibrations move from the center of the plate to the edges of the plate and then back, like ripples on a pond; because sound travels in a circular fashion and since the plate is usually rectangular, the reflections coming back from the edges add complexity to the vibration transmission patterns, creating a complex network of reflections which give the reverb a lush dense character; the decay time of the plate can be altered by adding damping material on its surface. Because of the way plate reverb works, it does not adequately mimic a reverberated sound in a physical space[19]; thus, plate reverbs are usually used to color a sound rather than to give it a sense of space.

The last standard kind of analog reverb is called a *spring reverb*; it works by replacing the metal sheet with a spring, the sound reverberating up and down the spring. The resulting sound is more metallic and usually needs to be shaped by EQ to sound more musical.

What parameters does a reverb use?

Reverb parameters are many, and of course change depending on the type of reverb, but here are a few. First, the early life of a reverb is described by how *early reflections* behave: this parameter describes how many and how strong they are; some reverb processors even allow you to define first and second reflections individually. Second, how reverb behaves in time (tail reverb) is defined with *pre-delay* (amount of time between the initial reverb and the appearance of tail end of the reverb), *decay time* (related to RT_{60}, see above; also sometimes called *damping*) and *diffusion* (how longer-lasting early reflections interact with the reverb tail). Other parameters allow the reverb to be shaped further: e.g. mid-side (or stereo width) allows controlling the dispersion of the reverb in the stereo field, or EQ filters can make the reverb brighter (low pass) or darker (high pass).

---

[19] See [18] to understand why

Flanger

A *flanger* is a type of delay where the delay changes with time.

This gives the characteristic "eeeaaaaaoooooaaaaaeeee" effect, like the phaser, but with more pronounced and deeper "eee" sounds than for the phaser; the sound of the effect is sometimes compared to a plane swooshing effect. Flanging sounds more natural to some people because the peaks obtained by adding a delayed version of a signal onto itself are evenly spaced (they are harmonically linked to the original frequencies). Flanging is used primarily for guitars, but can be used on any other instrument. You can find a list of recordings where flanging is prominent on Wikipedia.

Figure 12 Flanger The incoming signal goes through the splitter (S); one version of the signal is delayed before being recombined in the mixer (M) with the original signal; the amount of delay varies with time.

Chorus

A *chorus* mixes the original signal with a copy of itself that is both delayed and frequency shifted.

Figure 13 Chorus The incoming signal goes through the splitter (S); one version of the signal is delayed and frequency-shifted before being recombined in the mixer (M) with the original signal.

The frequency (or pitch) shifted signal is usually modulated with a *low frequency oscillator* (abbreviated *LFO*); this means that the increase or decrease in frequency of the original signal follows a sine-type wave with a low frequency. The result is a sound which appears to have multiple voices slightly different from one another; for example, "Pull me under" by Dream Theater has a clean chorus effect on the guitar at the beginning of the song.

2.7. Outboard Gear

What is outboard gear?
Depending on the taste and budget of the recording engineer, the amplified electrical tension, representing the signal containing our frequency information, can be directed to *outboard gear* to pre-process the signal before entering the digital domain through the Analog to Digital conversion (see Figure 5: the first box marked "P" is in fact the placeholder for outboard gear). It is called "outboard gear" to contrast with devices available "on/in the board" (mixing console) or, nowadays, with software available *in the box* (*ITB*), meaning on the computer. Note that outboard gear seems only to concern gear being used before the digital domain, even if technically speaking, whatever device is used after the digital domain also is outboard.

Some people put mic preamps in their outboard gear list. Although this is technically correct, I prefer to follow the logical signal path and talk about preamps just after microphones; from now on, whenever I mention outboard gear, this includes mic preamps

Should I use outboard gear?
Whether outboard gear should be used or not is a matter of personal preference. If you do not know exactly what you want to achieve when you are recording a sound source, leave the signal unprocessed for as long as possible: this will let you add or correct aspects of the sound later. If you do know what sound you are looking for and if you know how what you are currently hearing through monitoring will come out after layers and layers of processing, then pre-processing can be a very effective tool to gain time and energy in the mixing process later. Most professionals use outboard gear to pre-process the signal as a part of their "magic".

Compressors

Hardware compressors play a large part in how professional studios treat the analog sound. You will find a few models with their classical use in the table below[20]. Some of these hardware units have received the digital treatment and are available as plugins from various software companies. Do they sound as good as their original analog fathers? You will be the judge of that.

---

[20] See [20] and [21] for more on the topic

Maker	Model	Price	Use
API	2500	$2800	Drums, master bus
Art Pro Audio	Pro VLA II	$300	Color
Empirical Labs	EL8 Distressor	$1350	Drums
Fairchild	670	-	Vocals, drums
FMR Audio	RNC 1773	$200	Clean compression
Solid State Logic	XLogic G-Series	$4200	Master bus ("glue")
Summit	DCL200	$3150	Vocals
Teletronix	LA2A	$6500	Vocals, bass
Teletronix	LA3A	-	Vocals
Universal Audio	LA2A	$3500	Vocals, Teletronix LA2A clone
Universal Audio	2-1176	$2000	Vocals, UREI 1176 clone
Urei	1176	-	Vocals, drums, bass

Table 7 Hardware Compressors

Equalizer

Equalizers might not be everyone's first choice of outboard gear (preamps and compressors seem to be), but hardware EQs have their aficionados who will swear by them for their tone and coloring abilities. A few famous models are displayed in the table below, alongside more recent cheaper units.

Maker	Model	Price
API	550b	$1100
Ashly Audio	MQX-2310	$380
George Massenburg Labs	GML 8200	-
Kush Audio	Clariphonic Parallel EQ	$1600
Lang	PEQ2	$3300
Pultec	EQP1A3	$3700
Rane	ME 60S	$600
Speck Electronics	ASC-T	$600

Table 8 Hardware EQs

Chapter 3. In the Digital Domain

3.1. Analog to Digital Converter

Our signal is about to enter the magical realm of digital information. A lot of the concepts we will see in the coming pages are applicable to video because, in fact, what audio does with sound, video does with images: capture analog information and convert it into digital information for storage and manipulation. It all starts with the Analog to Digital converter.

If we summarize our signal path so far, we have created sound and captured it with a microphone. That is essentially it. All the "stuff" in between (mic preamp, outboard compressor, etc.) only serves the purposes of enhancing the signal one way or another.

How do I record the sound I captured?

But we have not recorded anything yet. The signal coming out of the microphone (or preamp, or outboard compressor, depending on your setup) would simply be lost forever. Sad, is it not? To make this story a bit less sad, we need to record this performance, or find a way to write this information somewhere so that we can retrieve it later. Nowadays, this is done on a computer called a *Digital Audio Workstation* (or *DAW*) which we will study in Section 3.2. Yes, I am ignoring the glory days of tape, cutters, serial delays and manual fader automation; lots of information about this topic can be found on the interwebz[21].

What is an analog to digital converter?

The problem is that computers do not speak electrical signals too well – they speak binary. So, we need to find a device to transform an electrical analog signal into a digital binary signal. That is exactly what an *analog to digital converter* (*AD converter*, also known as "A to D" or "AD") does: translate the analog frequency information contained in the electrical signal coming out of the analog domain into digital information which can be stored in the DAW's memory. Once it is stored, we have a choice of playing around with it (see Section 3.3) or replaying the sound (we will see how in Section 4.1).

---

[21] And also in [3]

Sampling Audio

What does sampling mean?

When an analog signal enters an AD converter, the converter measures the electrical voltage x times per second where x is the *sampling rate* (SR), usually expressed in Hz; a typical sampling rate of 44.1 kHz means that the voltage corresponding to the incoming audio will be measured 44100 times per second. Each of these measures is called a *sample*. A sampling rate of x Hz can only accurately reproduce a sound of maximal frequency of $\frac{x}{2}$: this is the Nyquist frequency; for example, a 44-kHz sampling rate can only accurately reproduce signals with frequencies lower than 20 kHz.

Why not 22 kHz? Because the filtering off has a slope (in dB/oct., exactly like an EQ filter) and will take some time to cancel the signal 100%. This is the Nyquist-Shannon theorem, famous in information theory; you need at least two sampling points per cycle to accurately reconstruct a sine wave: a sine wave cycle is the time difference between two points having the same amplitude! What is hidden behind this seemingly trivial assertion is the fact that we can exactly reproduce an incoming analog signal using a finite amount of digital information!

Aliasing, jitter: what are they?

If the sampling rate is too low, e.g. sampling at 16 kHz for a 12-kHz sound, *aliasing* will occur: when reconstructing the waveform from the sampled points on the way out, the resulting wave would have a lower frequency than the original because sampling with less points than 2 per cycle gives you a signal with a lower frequency[22]. The remedy? An *anti-aliasing* filter, like an EQ low pass filter, starting at the Nyquist frequency to cut off any greater frequencies in the signal.

How does the converter know that it is sampling at 44100 times per second? It does because it uses a reference (usually called a clock, go figure) to know how accurately it is sampling. Why is this important? Well, imagine what happens if, on the way out (digital to analog conversion, or DA), the clock used to reconstruct the signal is not exactly synced with the in-sampling clock? *Jitter* will occur: voltage (analog) values will be assigned to bit (digital) values at a slightly incorrect moment with respect to its

---

[22] See [22] for details, with a very nice graphical rendition of the phenomenon

intended time placement; this will distort the sound and add harshness described in many articles about jitter[23].

There is however a case to be made that jitter cannot be perceived by most people in a standard non-high-end listening environment. The higher quality of converters in mass-consumption electronics might be another reason why complaints about jitter are not any louder than what they are.

3.2. Audio Interface

Now that we have converted our signal into discrete (separate) bits of binary information, we are ready to start playing with it, right? Right - but where does this conversion physically happen? Where is the AD converter? That is where the *audio interface* comes in (if you are using outboard AD converters, you should not be reading this book ☺).

What is an audio interface?
The audio interface is simply a bundle of audio components, most of which we have already discussed. However, because they are so pervasive in home and project studios, and because their accessibility (both in terms of price and required technical expertise) is a large part of what has made audio more widespread, audio interfaces deserve a section of their own.

An audio interface can either take the form of an audio PCI-type card to insert into your favorite computer, or of a separate hardware unit connected to a computer via USB, Firewire or some other means. In its simplest form, the audio interface is an AD converter and a DA converter. In higher-end models, it can also contain components such as mic preamps, EQ filters, compressors, MIDI input and output connectors, etc.

If we look at Figure 14, we have a single microphone connected to the audio interface (white box), usually via an XLR connection. Within that audio interface, a microphone pre-amplifier adds gain to the signal so that it can be properly processed by the AD converter. Out of the AD converter go the bits corresponding to the analog signal captured by the microphone, and into the output of the audio interface (the DAW), usually via a USB or Firewire connection. Once the signal is stored, it can be played back by reconstructing the analog information from the digital information in the DA

---

[23] See [23] and [24] for details

converter, and then out of the audio interface into the speakers, usually via an XLR or jack connection.

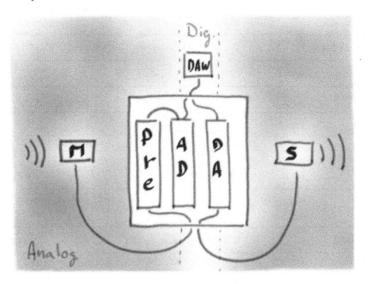

Figure 14 Simple Audio Interface Internal Logic *A microphone (M) picks up incoming sound. The cable connecting the microphone to the audio interface transports the analog signal into a preamplifier (Pre). The signal is converted into a digital signal by the AD converter, then comes out of the audio interface and is sent to the DAW for processing. Finally, it goes back into the interface into the DA converter before being sent out of the interface to a speaker (S). Note how the audio interface carries its name well: it bridges the analog (dark) and digital (light) domains.*

I want to buy an audio interface, help me!

As you can see in Figure 14, the audio interface is the central device in this example. It acts as the go-between between the analog domain (dark grey) and digital domain (white). You will find in the table below some famous audio interfaces for home or project studios. The pros usually use larger units such as consoles.

Most of those listed below connect to your computer via USB or Firewire (the name given by Apple to the IEEE1394 norm), and all of them provide Phantom Power except the Lexicon Alpha. The "A/D" column specifies the characteristics of the A/D converter in terms of its bit depth (in bits) and sampling rate (in kHz), in that order; see Section 3.3 for details. The "Input" and "Output" columns list the inputs and outputs for the interface (¼" = ¼ inch TRS, C = Combo connector, allowing both ¼" TRS and XLR).

Vendor	Model	Price	A/D	MIDI	Input	Output
Apogee	Duet	$600	24/192	Via USB	2xC	3x¼"
Avid	FastTrack Duo	$140	24/48	No	2xC 2x¼"	3x¼"
Focusrite	Scarlett 2i2	$150	24/96	No	2xC	3x¼"
Lexicon	Alpha	$50	24/48	No	3x¼" 1xXLR	2xRCA 3x¼"
M-Audio	M-Track Plus II	$150	24/96	No	2xC	3x¼"
Mackie	Onyx Blackbird	$500	24/96	No	8xC 2x¼" 8xADAT	8x¼" 8xADAT
MOTU	Ultralite MK3	$550	24/192	In, Out	2xC 6x¼" 1xS/PDIF	10x¼" 1xS/PDIF
Presonus	FireStudio Project	$400	24/96	In, Out	8xC 2x¼" 1xS/PDIF	13x¼" 1xS/PDIF
Roland	Quad Capture	$250	24/192	In, Out	2xC 1xS/PDIF	3x¼" 1xS/PDIF
Steinberg	UR 22	$150	24/192	In, Out	2xC	3x¼"

Table 9 Audio Interfaces

For each microphone (XLR or combo) input connector there is a corresponding microphone preamp in the unit. The quality of the preamps is one of the factors influencing the price of the unit, but not the only one: other factors include, in no order, the number of connectors, the quality of the AD and DA converters, the presence of digital meters and the inclusion of a MIDI input and/or output connector.

3.3. Digital Audio Workstation

What is a digital audio workstation?

The Digital Audio Workstation (DAW) is the brain of the audio system: it stores the digitized sound; it feeds information to software plugins for digital processing; it then feeds bit music to the DA converter to transform the processed digital information back into analog voltages.

The DAW, from a technical point of view, is a computer (hardware and operating system) with specialized processing software installed on it. The audio interface drivers are technically part of the operating system: you could say that the audio interface extends onto the DAW, but that would not make things any clearer, would it?

When they speak about a DAW, most people mean the processing software itself rather than the whole system, most likely because hardware is so ubiquitous these days. Before you ask, both PCs and Macs are worthy choices for DAW hardware.

I want to buy a DAW, help me!

In the table below, the most popular DAWs are presented. I am not going into the "which one is better" debate because, frankly, it is pointless: do I argue about what socks you should be wearing?

Vendor	Name	Version	Price	Main selling points
Sony	**Acid Pro**	--	$150	Focus on composing & looping
--	**Audacity**	--	Free	Free entry-level recording
Steinberg	**Cubase**[24]	Elements Artist Pro	$100 $300 $550	Included instruments, focus on creation
Ableton	**Live**[25]	Intro Standard Suite	$90 $390 $660	Focus on producing & performing
Apple	**Logic Pro**	--	$200	Included instruments
Steinberg	**Nuendo**	--	$1800	Post-production expert
Avid	**Pro Tools**[26]	First --	Free $600	Audio industry standard
Cockos	**Reaper**	--	$60[27]	Configurability, included plugins
Cakewalk	**Sonar**[28]	Artist Professional Platinum	$99 $199 $499	Ease of use, included plugins
PreSonus	**StudioOne**[29]	Prime Artist Professional	Free $200 $400	Included effect plugins

Table 10 Mixing Software (DAW)

How do I work with a DAW?

Working with modern DAWs is usually very easy: you start by recording tracks directly from the audio interface, or by importing tracks (usually in uncompressed WAV format) into the software. Arranging the tracks in some logical manner should be the next step: modern productions can

---

[24] See [25] for a comparison
[25] See [26] for a comparison
[26] See [27] for a comparison; Pro Tools Express can only be acquired in a bundle with other Avid products such as audio interfaces; Avid also proposes a subscription model
[27] $225 if you make more than $20'000 per year with the software
[28] See [28] for a comparison; Cakewalk also proposes a subscription model
[29] See [29] for a comparison

contain over 100 tracks, the norm being in the 50-70 tracks range. Labelling, giving tracks a color, grouping tracks by instrument type – these methods help make sense of the structure of the recording. Routing information from one track to another, or from one track group (*bus*) to another, helps minimize the logical signal path.

Once that is done, the tracks can be mixed: a balance must be found between these instruments and voices. Some elements need to be refocused or corrected with the list of effects described in Section 2.5: gates, reverbs, compressors, EQ, etc. Anything works, if it sounds good. These effects are usually associated to a track in the form of a software *plugin* in one of many formats, the most well-known being *VST* (Virtual Studio Technology, developed by Steinberg) and *AAX* (Avid Audio Extension, developed by... Avid). Once the balance is found and all the elements in the mix have been properly taken advantage of, a portable version of the mix is exported to an audio file so that it can be distributed and consumed.

Storing Audio

What is the bit depth?
The data captured from the sampling described in Section 3.1 is digitally stored in numbers represented by bits. The total number of bits available to store the information contained in each sample is the *bit depth BD*; the larger the bit depth, the more amplitudes of that sample can be recorded and stored; note that the bit depth does not impact the accuracy of the signal's sampling: that is the job of the sampling rate.

What is the dynamic range?
What the bit depth has an influence on is the maximum loudness of a signal, represented by the *dynamic range* (DR_{max}) or *signal to noise ratio* SNR of the signal:

$$DR_{max} \sim 6 * BD$$

Equation 8 Dynamic Range and Bit Depth

For a 16-bit system $(BD = 16)$, $DR_{max} \sim 96\,dB$. For a 24-bit system, $DR_{max} \sim 144\,dB$. The dynamic range represents the height of the sampling window: whatever is larger cannot be sampled accurately. The raging debate about which bit depth should be used (16 vs. 24 bits) can be put to rest with simple comparison tests: listen to a song at 16 bits and then at 24 bits. I can guarantee you that most people will not hear the difference - but everyone still uses a 24-bit depth, including me: you never know ☺

What does 0 dB FS mean?

One note of importance: most DAWs will show you sound "volume" in dB FS (for Full Scale) with a negative value. Why? Because 0 *dB FS* is defined as the maximum capacity (the bit depth) of the AD converter; thus, any sound will have a negative value (lower than 0 which is the maximum).

What happens when you work at 24 bits but then decide to export your file at 16 bits? We are losing information, are we not? And that is bad because losing information means losing the possibility to reconstruct the original sound without artifacts and distortions, right? Yes, but there is a way around the problem. A technique called *dithering* uses the fact that our ears are very good a picking out individual frequencies from a sound but bad at picking out random noise at many frequencies: dithering mixes in random noise into the original sound to fake our ears into thinking every bit of information is there. This process is also used when moving up the bit-depth ladder instead of down.

Audio Bandwidth

What is audio bandwidth?

Audio bandwidth is the amount of audio data passing through some device; it is expressed in kbps (for kilobits per second, or 1024 bits per second) and is called the *bit-rate BR* :

$$BR = BD * SR * MS$$

Equation 9 Bit Rate

where BD is the bit depth, SR is the sampling rate and MS is a mono/stereo variable (mono: $MS = 1$, stereo $MS = 2$). Standard CD sound is usually stereo ($MS = 2$) and transmitted in packets of 16 bits ($BD = 16$) at 44.1 kHz ($SR = 44100$), giving a bit-rate BR of = 1411.2 kbps. At that standard rate, a 3-minute (180 seconds) song would be large at 260 Mb, or 32.5 MB (1 Byte = 8 bits).

What does MP3 mean?

At the time when digital audio started to become popular with the use of CDs, network bandwidth and disk sizes were not large enough for files that size to be practical. Thus, audio files were compressed. *Compression* is the process by which the amount of information used to represent (or encode) a file is decreased. Lossy compression is the same process but with loss of information. For example, the popular MP3 format is the result of lossy compression (MP3 means **MP**EG-1 or MPEG-2 Audio Layer **3).** The technique used is based upon an effect called *masking*: a weaker sound is masked by a louder sound at similar frequencies; this means that instead of representing the information of both sounds in the file, only the information of the louder sound is encoded in the file.

Standard MP3 usually has a bit rate of 128 kbps; that is 10 times less than what our calculation above has come up with! But with that bit-rate, the song size is also divided by 10, which gives the standard 3 MB per song. With a standard 16-bit audio system, that is a sampling rate of 4 kHz in stereo. Compare this to the CD standard sampling rate of 44.1 kHz and you will understand why certain people consider MP3-style compression an aberration.

Is it good enough for you? Only your ears can decide. Note that MP3 encoders can vary depending on the algorithms used; also, MP3 file formats allow bit rates up to 320 kbps to be used. With bigger bandwidth and larger storage capacities available, audiophiles prefer to listen to music encoded in *lossless compression* formats such as FLAC (Free Lossless Audio Codec) which can reduce the size of an audio file by 50-60% without altering its quality.

Latency

What is latency?

We know that a converter creates samples by measuring the incoming electrical voltage. As it works through the signal, the converter places the samples in a temporary memory location called a *buffer*. When the buffer is full, the computer retrieves all the stored data in one operation to process it. The reason for this mechanism is that the computer might be busy doing other things as it is processing the signal; if it is too busy, it might miss certain samples, introducing distortion artifacts in the rendered sound; imagine a factory worker putting pieces in a box: if the conveyor belt moves too fast, the worker will miss certain pieces. The *latency* L can be calculated as follows:

$$L = \frac{BS}{SR}$$

Equation 10 Latency

where BS is the buffer size (number of samples). Therefore, you will hear audio engineers say: "Man, this buffer size is total BS".

Why do I care about latency?

For example, a fast computer might accommodate a buffer size of 64 samples for a sampling rate of 44.1 kHz since the latency produced will be about 1.5 ms (64 / 44100 = 0.00145 seconds, or 1.45 milliseconds). A slower computer might need 512 samples to avoid distortion, but this would generate a latency of about 11ms, which can be an issue if you are recording drums with a click track, for example. You can increase the sampling rate, thus reducing the latency; for example, a 512 buffer size with a sampling rate of 96 kHz produces a latency of about 5ms.

In turn, increasing the sampling rate might force the computer into missing some samples, thereby introducing the infamous distortion. ASIO (Audio Stream Input Output) drivers allow you change the buffer size on the fly; this change can be expressed in latency terms; for example, you could set your buffer size to "high latency" for slower computers. Do you know which company invented ASIO drivers? Steinberg. Again? Yes, Steinberg was a huge player in the early developments of audio technology.

The time it takes for a computer to sample the incoming sound is in direct relation with its computing capacity (its processing speed). With a "slow" computer, the buffer size must be larger. If you try to reduce the buffer size, cracking noises will appear. The best way to strike a balance is to experiment with various settings, buy a faster computer, or outsource the computing to outboard gear.

3.4. MIDI

What is MIDI?

We take a small detour from our signal path. So far, the sound has been produced and recorded in the DAW. It might have been processed, changed, altered, or modified. Or not. But what if you want to add another instrument? Say that you wanted to add a flute to a song you are working on but you cannot play that instrument. Composing music is one thing, and playing that composition with all the planned instruments is another. A *Musical Instrument Digital Interface* (MIDI) might prove useful in this case: it will allow you to create sounds representing any instrument from a MIDI instrument called a *controller*. You need three things to make it work: someone performing with the controller, a way to communicate between the controller and the computer, and a sound representing the desired instrument, stored on the computer.

The first item is taken care of very easily: you can buy MIDI controllers for dirt cheap, or even ask your smartphone to do it for you. The most common type of controller is the keyboard-type controller. There are also wind-type MIDI controllers, allowing for a very rich range of note expressions. Percussion controllers allow you to play drums on a "real" instrument and modify the drum sounds later.

The second item is where MIDI comes in. MIDI is a messaging standard which communicates note information digitally. Amongst others, MIDI messages contain the following items: note number, note velocity, note on timing, note off timing, volume, pitch-bend and channel (16 channels maximum). Notes range from C1 (around 8 Hz) to G9 (12.5 kHz). This information can be encapsulated in a file with the *SMF* (*Standard Midi File*) format. Where is the instrument information? It is not included in MIDI. MIDI only contains note information, not instrument information. A lot of people associate MIDI with 80s video game music sounds: that is only because computers have a very basic set of sounds in their sound library, so when played with default PC settings, MIDI sounds awful.

How do I use MIDI?

However, and that is where the third item comes in, sound libraries (also called *sample libraries*) nowadays contain hundreds of thousands of sounds, from percussion to strings to guitars to voices to winds to special effects. If it can be recorded, it can be sampled. The process of creating these samples is extremely time-consuming: you record each sound multiple times in various conditions so that when it is played by the computer, it sounds like a real instrument. In the more expensive sample libraries, you even find the same instruments played in different manners, like for example a violin played pizzicato or a guitar played muted. The only thing you need is a piece of software to play those samples per the MIDI information contained in the MIDI data transmitted from the controller – yet another use for your DAW.

This is how you would create that flute track in your song. First, get a MIDI controller and hook it into your audio interface – that is why some of them have a MIDI IN connector. Second, open your DAW of choice, add a track and prepare it for recording. Third, perform the flute part on the MIDI controller while recording it on the computer through the DAW. What happens if you now press the play button in your DAW? Nothing. Why? You have not told the DAW with what instrument it needs to play those recorded MIDI notes. Add a sample-playing plugin to the track, select the instrument *et voilà*, you now have a flute leading the way in your Swedish death funk song.

The power of MIDI resides in the fact that it is very flexible: you can use it with any DAW, with any MIDI controller, with any sample library. You could also buy a computer or smartphone application to generate MIDI notes (and music scores!) for you – if the format described above is respected, you are good to go. Because sample libraries are recorded so well, it is becoming increasingly difficult to tell a sample from the real thing. There are exceptions, of course (stringed and wind instruments come to mind), but for most intents and purposes, a single sample will do just fine.

Chapter 4. From Digital Audio to Analog Sound

4.1. Digital to Analog Converter

Here we are. Our trip comes to an end. The recorded sound travelled first through a microphone membrane to generate electrical impulses, then through various cables and electronic components, into a converter to transform the analog signal into a digital signal so that the power of computers can be used to work on the sound; the signal must then pass through another converter (see below) before being transformed into moving air molecules by another transducer like a speaker (Section 4.2) to finish its journey in our ears (Section 4.4). We will make a short journey through acoustics to understand why that is important when we listen to sounds in a physical space like a room (Section 4.3).

Digitized information is now ready to be sent from the DAW to a *Digital to Analog* (DA) converter - this is the DA converter role depicted in Figure 5. DA converters can be found in PC sound cards, MP3 players, audio interfaces and standalone devices.

Why do we need a DA converter?
Simply because our ears cannot hear digital information too well. Our ears need air molecules pushing against our internal eardrum. That is in the analog domain, so we need to send our digital information through a DA converter.

Remember the Nyquist-Shannon theorem from page 57? We know that we can reconstruct a signal with the same quality as the original signal. A typical DA converter works like this: it transforms the discrete step-like digital (virtual) signal into a discrete step-like physical signal by producing an electrical impulse each time a bit of data passes through; the voltage of that electrical impulse is kept constant until the next bit of data passes through. Interpolation techniques allow this constant voltage to be changed into more continuous signals by having the DA converter guess what the original voltage might have been. A low-pass reconstruction filter is used to weed out frequency artifacts. DA converters possess the same characteristics as their AD cousins: bit-depth, sampling rate, dynamic range; they are subjected to the same problems as well (jitter, noise, etc.).

4.2. Speakers

Now that the signal is back in the green analog domain of in the form of electrical voltages, we can get some air molecules to move by placing another set of electro-acoustic transducers in the signal path: speakers.

How do speakers work?

Speakers are essentially plastic cones moving back and forth at the frequency of the sounds present in the signal. This is how it works: the plastic cone moves under the influence of a mobile electromagnet attached to it; that mobile electromagnet moves under the influence of a fixed permanent magnet attached to the speaker box. Whenever an electrical signal gets into the speaker, the permanent magnet generates a magnetic field which causes the mobile electromagnet to move; whenever the electrical signal's sign is changed (it does since the electrical tension behaves like a sine wave), the direction of the magnetic field is reversed, causing the electromagnet to move in the opposite direction[30]; as a result, the electromagnet (and the cone) move back and forth, creating compression and rarefaction zones at the wavelength of the electrical signal.

The amplitude of the cone movement determines the volume of the sound produced. Low frequencies are reproduced with heavy driver material like plastic, while higher frequencies need lighter material like silk to move a lot faster under the influence of the moving electromagnet. Speakers, headphones and ear buds all work in the manner described above; the only difference between them is the size of the components[31].

What kind of speakers or headphones do audio engineers use?

Contrary to audiophiles or the everyday music listener, audio engineers want the sound to be reproduced with the highest possible fidelity to the signal as it enters the transducing system. I just said "highest fidelity" which reads HiFi for most people. The irony is that most HiFi systems are not designed with the highest fidelity in mind; instead, they aim at giving the listener the best possible experience by modifying the sound before it comes out of the speakers; it is not uncommon to place amplifiers and other devices like equalizers between the DA converter and the transducer. Even if there is no device physically placed in the chain, speaker manufacturers

---

[30] There is a very nice model of this in [30]
[31] See the pictures in [31]

will include signal processing inside the speakers to give you a "warm and inviting sound", or "the punchiest mid-range you have ever heard".

Of course, when you are trying to mix a song with your DAW, you want your sound to be portable to any kind of listening environment: a nice HiFi system, a car audio system, headphones, one ear bud, a club dance floor, crappy PC speakers, etc. If you mix your song on a speaker system that does not reproduce the signal that is in fact coming in, you will add features to your sound which will not *translate* well to other systems; a typical example of this is mixing on bad headphones: because these tend to lack bass frequencies, you add more into your mix; you then listen in your car (car systems typically overemphasize bass frequencies) and what comes out of your car stereo is a herd of rumbling elephants; yes, that is personal experience right there.

Audio engineers want to use a transducing system which very reliably gives back whatever comes out of the DA converter with as little distortion as possible: this is called having a *flat frequency response*. This flat response feature is desirable in both speakers and headphones for audio engineering. The process of listening to audio sounds as you are mixing them is called *monitoring*, so monitoring speakers are called studio monitors, or *monitors* for short.

Something else which audio engineers like to know before buying their monitors is the range of frequencies that the speaker system can reproduce. Even if the human hearing range is known to be approximately 20 Hz to 20 kHz, certain manufacturers insist on producing speakers whose range extend (far) beyond 20 kHz. Most good monitoring systems are built to reproduce frequency ranges from about 40 Hz to right above 20 kHz. Most speakers have either female XLR or TRS inputs, or both. They sometimes include *trim switches* to take away some volume, either on the low end or the high end or both; they sometimes also include EQ shelf switches.

The power delivered by monitoring speakers is usually lower than that of loudspeakers: the goal is not to deafen you, but to give you the most accurate sonic representation of the outgoing signal. In fact, audio engineers can sometimes suffer from hearing fatigue or even hearing loss if they work at sound pressure levels which are too high. A good starting point is to listen at 80-85 dB SPL; some engineers say that you should be able to speak over music being played by studio monitors without raising your voice. Either way, listening at quiet levels is beneficial both short and long term.

We have talked a lot about flat frequency response. If you ever do a comparison between speaker models, or go to monitor manufacturer websites, you will not always find frequency response data. The reason for this is simple: the flattest response is not always very flat, which means that the standard user going to buy monitors looking at a wiggly frequency response graph will think the manufacturer is lying to them. Before buying speakers based on manufacturer data, check out tests and frequency response graphs from independent testers if you can find them[32].

I want to buy good monitors, help me!

In the next table, I have listed famous monitors, or at least monitors people talk about. They are all decent studio monitors, some very good; I have tried to list flagship-style monitors from each company, but of course, all the manufacturers cited produce other models, available on their respective websites. These monitors are studio monitors, not Hi-Fi monitors: the goal is to reproduce, not to dazzle.

Vendor	Model	Price	Frequency response	Drivers LF/HF	Power LF/HF [W]	Out [dB SPL]
Adam	A7x	$1000	42 – 50	7"/1.5"	100/50	114
Dynaudio	BM5 mkIII	$1200	42 – 24	7"/1.1"	50/50	118
Equator Audio	D5	$400	53 – 20	5.25"/1"	50/50	103
Event	Opal	$3000	35 – 22	7.1"/1"	270/50	114
Focal	Twin6 Be	$3700	40 – 40	6.5"/1"	300/100	115
Genelec	M040	$1600	48 – 20	6.5"/1"	80/50	107
JBL	LSR305	$300	43 – 24	5"/1"	41/41	108
KRK	Rokit 5 G3	$300	45 – 35	5"/1"	30/20	106
M-Audio	BX5 D2	$180	56 – 22	5"/1"	40/30	100
Mackie	HR824mk2	$1400	37 – 20	8.75"/1"	150/100	111
Neumann	KH120	$1500	52 – 21	5.25"/1"	50/50	111
Presonus	Eris E5	$300	53 – 22	5.25"/1"	45/35	102
Yamaha	HS8	$700	38 – 30	8"/1"	75/45	--

Table 11 Studio Monitors

---

[32] There is more frequency response magic at [32]

The price column indicates the price for a pair of monitors since most of us have two ears. The frequency response column gives the lowest possible frequency produced by the subwoofer (the first number, in Hz) and the highest possible frequency produced by the tweeter (the second number, in kHz). The "drivers" column gives driver diameters in inches: LF for Low Frequency, HF for High Frequency. The power column gives the maximum power available at low (LF) and high (HF) frequencies.

All the monitors listed above are of the same type: 2-way near-field monitors. *2-way* means that the speaker has two drivers; if you remember the last time you saw studio pictures, you will notice that most monitors have two sets of cones – two sets of drivers. Why? Because remember, you need different materials to create air waves with different frequency ranges; some speakers even have three drivers to use the best possible materials. The low frequency driver is called the *subwoofer* and is typically 5 to 8 inches in size; the high frequency driver is called the *tweeter* and is typically about 1 inch in size.

The issue with the multiple driver system is that at some point in the frequency range, both drivers would move air, which is not desirable because it would introduce interferences and artifacts in the produced sound. A *crossover frequency* is defined : just below that frequency, the subwoofer starts to fade out and the tweeter takes over. Of course, the way the system handles that crossover is critical for a truly flat frequency response. *Near-field* means that the monitors are meant to be used for listening at close ranges and are not meant for concerts.

4.3. Acoustics

We now have speakers to recreate airwaves from the transduced signal coming out of the DAW. Awesome. We are sitting in our room, listening, and it sounds awful. Why? Because the sound interacts with the room walls, ceiling and floor, creating interferences and all sorts of artefacts that are on a mission to destroy the flat response that your $10'000 speakers are sending to your ears.

Three phenomena describe what happens when sound bounces around your room:

- *Diffraction*: what happens when sound passes through openings or around a barrier
- *Refraction*: what happens when the sound changes medium
- *Reflection*: what happens when the sound bounces off room surfaces

Diffraction

From general wave theory, we know that diffraction is what helps waves bend around corners and openings. The amount of diffraction is proportional to wavelength; this means that it is inversely proportional to frequency: the lower the frequency, the larger the diffraction effect. This is the reason why owls can be heard through large distances in a forest, while other birds with higher-pitched chirps struggle to get their voice heard over such distances: diffraction counters the attenuation effect described in Section 1.1.

When the wavelength is smaller than the opening, there is no observable effect: the airwave is "too small". An open window might have an opening dimension of about 1 meter (~3 feet); a sound with a much smaller wavelength (say 20 cm or about 8 inches) has a frequency of about 1715 Hz: anything around or above that will not exhibit any diffraction effect.

For our purposes, diffraction effects are important basically only in microphones: how does the microphone enclosure diffract the incoming sound? We want as little diffraction as possible so that no interferences can be created between the incoming and diffracted sound, even though you could argue that diffraction patterns are what is giving some microphones their "color".

Refraction / Absorption

Refraction is what happens when a wave changes medium, for example when the sound produced by one of your speakers hits a wall. Wave theory tells us that when refraction happens, the speed of propagation and the wavelength change but not the frequency (see Equation 2 to remind yourself why). The logical consequence is that the sound waves hitting the wall will keep its frequency (would it not be fun if it were not the case?) and continue its path through a much denser medium; with what we know from

Section 1.1, this means that the sound will be attenuated "into the wall" and mostly not come out on the other side (except for those pesky low frequencies). This process is also called *absorption* and plays a very large part in our rooms and studios.

Reflection

The last phenomenon we want to discuss is the most important one: reflection is what happens when a wave bounces off a surface.

Why do I care about sound reflection?

A wave bouncing off room walls will behave differently depending on the size of the room. I will take walls as my generic example, but everything is also true for ceilings, floors and any other obstacle. If the wavelength is right around the distance between our walls or any of its multiples, reflections will create a *standing wave* by bouncing off the wall and recombining with the original sound. If, on the other hand, the wavelength is much shorter than the room dimensions, then we can consider airwaves to be very directional like rays of light and use basic geometry to figure out where the sound goes.

Imagine a 34.3 cm long air wave; its frequency is 1 kHz: from Equation 2, we have 343 / 0.343 = 1000: this bounces nicely in a standard 3 by 4-meter room (roughly a 1 ft. wave in a 10x13 ft. room). Now go to 100 Hz: the wave is 3.43 meters long, which is almost exactly the size of the room I just mentioned – how does a wave bounce back and forth in those conditions? Note that when people say that bass frequencies are not directional, that is what they mean: low frequencies cannot bounce around because of their size, while higher frequencies can (and do).

Why do people say that bass frequencies build up in corners?

To understand why, we must remember that a sound wave represents the various changes in air pressure; basic physics tell us that at a boundary (e.g. a wall), the speed of those changes will be zero (the airwave speed is zero at the wall; this sounds logical, the wall is not moving) while the pressure there will be maximal. An angle is the junction of two boundaries (or surfaces), and a corner is the junction of three boundaries: pressure will be respectively double and triple that of the surface! That is where the buildup comes from.

Sound as Standing Waves

What is a room mode?
Let us go back to standing waves. Because the formation of standing waves in a room depends on the room's dimensions, you could say that the room has acoustical properties which are going to induce those standing waves; that is why standing waves are sometimes called room *modes*. Technically speaking, a mode is an energy satisfying the standing waves boundary condition of the general wave equation, but it is easier to speak about room modes. Let us imagine a wave bouncing between two walls (see Figure 3): the first standing wave will have nulls at the wall positions; the second standing wave will have nulls at the walls and right in the middle (second harmonic), and so on.

We can calculate the frequency of these standing waves v_{SW} with Equation 2 for a room with distance d between two surfaces, the n standing wave frequencies will be

$$v_{SW} = \frac{c}{2 * d} * n$$

Equation 11 Standing Wave Frequencies

where c is the speed of sound. The factor 2 accounts for the fact that a full wave cycle is from one surface to the other and back, not just from one surface to the other. For example, a room with one side measuring 4 m (about 13 feet) will have a first harmonic room mode ($n = 1$) at about 43 Hz, a second harmonic mode at about 86 Hz, etc. A much larger room of 8 m (about 26 feet) will have its first mode at 21.5 Hz, the second at 43 Hz, etc. You already see that larger rooms are better in the sense that their first room mode will be below our hearing threshold, but since larger is usually more expensive, you must strike a balance between size and cost for your listening space.

Which of my room modes has the lowest frequency?
Looking at Equation 11, we see that the room dimension is in the denominator; this means that if we take the largest side of our room for d, we will find our lowest mode. That is what I have calculated above for a room with a 4-meter (13 foot) length: the first mode will be at 43 Hz. This means that if you would be interested in playing 20 Hz sounds (from a subwoofer, for example), you would not need to worry about your room's

dimensions. Why? 20 Hz corresponds to a wave with a wavelength of about 17 meters; our room would have to be about 8.5 meters long for this to become a problem.

Why do I care about room modes?

Do these modes complicate our lives all the way up to our 20-kHz hearing limit? They do but they don't, and here is why. Our listening space is three-dimensional; thus, a room will have different *modes* along each direction depending on how the sound bounces around. First, the most important and more intense, the *axial modes*; these are modes where sound is reflected between two opposing surfaces (like what is shown in Figure 3. Second, *tangential modes*: they involve two sets of parallel surfaces (four surfaces) and are about half as intense as the axial modes. Finally, the *oblique modes* are the least intense of the three, where sound bounces off all three sets of opposing surfaces[33]. Let us see what kind of frequencies these modes have.

We can generalize Equation 11 into an equation valid in case of real space in three dimensions:

$$v_{SW}^{l,w,h} = \frac{c}{2} * \sqrt{\left(\frac{l}{L}\right)^2 + \left(\frac{w}{W}\right)^2 + \left(\frac{h}{H}\right)^2}$$

Equation 12 Standing Wave Frequencies for a Three-dimensional Space

where c is the speed of sound, l, w, h are the numbers representing the modes (like n in the one-dimensional case) and L, W, H are the room dimensions. Let us take a 4 by 3 by 2-meter room and calculate the lowest mode (13 by 10 by 6.5 feet). My largest dimension here is L, and we know that axial modes are the more intense (the more annoying); this means that $l = 1, w = 0, h = 0$. We nicely fall back on our previous calculation: 43 Hz! What you see is that you can very easily calculate your room modes in an excel spreadsheet. If you do, you will get all your room modes, up to whatever l, w, h you want. The trick is that room modes are only relevant up to a certain range of frequencies because past that region, airwaves start to behave like light and bounce around like light rays. I say "region"

---

[33] You can find very nice drawings of these modes in [33]

because the change in behavior (from standing wave to light ray) does not happen dramatically.

What is the Davis frequency?
If you want to know up to what point you need to calculate your room modes, pick $l, w, h = 5$. This normally coincides with the Davis frequency:

$$v_{Davis} = \frac{3*c}{L_{min}}$$

Equation 13 Davis Frequency

where L_{min} is the smallest dimension of your room[34]. A lot of people mistakenly reference the Schroeder frequency here; this is wrong because Schroeder's work specifically targeted large acoustic spaces; we are not in a large acoustic space, unless you live in a mansion, that is. In the case we are discussing, v_{Davis}= 515 Hz and the $l, w, h = 5$ mode is at 520 Hz: both give us approximately the same limit.

There are lots of nice room mode calculators on the internet[35], so head over there and try out your room: where are your main modes? If it so happens that your room is square, look out: each axial mode will ring twice as loud! That is the reason why cinema and studio rooms are never square by design. Another thing to look for is modes bunched up together forming clusters: their intensities will add up and become more troublesome. How close? Closer to 5% from each other; I read the 5% number in several places but could not figure out an accurate source.

Sound as Light Rays
If we now turn to the higher frequency case (say anything beyond 500 Hz for our test case), sound waves behave like rays of light: we are in the realm of geometry. Sound will bounce off walls multiple times before fading out, having lost some energy after each hit. Because of the way our ears work (see Section 4.4), we want the sound coming out of the speakers to reach our ears before any of the pesky reflections we just talked about.

What is interesting is that sound delayed by less than 1 ms helps our brain determine the location of the source of the sound, so those reflections are in fact useful: source location is related to sound imaging, also called stereo

---

[34] See [34]
[35] For example, see [35], or [36] for a nice graphical representation

imaging. If we move up the ladder to between 1 and 50 ms, our brain will lump those reflections with the original sound, so they are no danger because we will not perceive them. Reflections coming between 50 and 400 ms after the initial sound will give the sound a cavernous quality; after 400 ms, reflections will be heard as separate sounds, also called *echoes*[36]. First conclusion: any reflection with more than 50 ms delay with respect to the original sound needs to be eliminated.

What is the sweet spot?
Because of reflection, the sound travels further. Some waves coming back from reflection will cross the path of waves moving in the opposite direction; this will produce interferences and reshape the sound: in some locations, frequencies will add up, and in some others, they will cancel out. This means that depending on where you are listening from, the sound will not be the same.

This is where the notion of *sweet spot* comes from: taking the geometry of the room and speaker placement into account, there are better spots than others for a good listening experience. If the sweet spot is large, moving around it will not dramatically alter the listening experience; if it is smaller, the sound will change even if you move your head a few inches. This is of course true for any listening environment, not just a home studio: in front of your TV, in your car, etc. You can measure the acoustic properties of your room; it takes a bit of time and money but is well worth it[37].

Dealing with Reflection: Absorption

How does absorption work?
We are going to use absorption to deal with the reflection we want to get rid of. How? Remember Equation 7? RT_{60} measures the time it takes for sound to decrease its intensity by 60 dB; V is the volume of the room, S is the total surface area of the room and a is the average absorption coefficient of the material of the room surfaces. With everything we just discovered, we want RT_{60} to be as small as possible, which means that we want the absorption to be as large as possible.

Airwaves absorption depends on the frequency of the sound, as demonstrated by the absorption tables you can find on the internet. Do not

---

[36] See [37]
[37] You can check [38] for details

fret, I have done the work for you: for general material absorption, see [39]; for rock & glass wool, see [40]. Thus, putting blankets up in your recording space will tame high frequency reflections (yes it will, see the tables I just mentioned), but will do almost nothing to prevent lower frequencies creating happy standing waves, causing this booming sound feared by all home studio owners. This means that if you want to tame the lower room modes (typically our 43 Hz mode for example), you must put a fair amount of material in its path.

How do I get rid of unwanted reflections?
So what should we do? The standard answer is: "It depends". And it does. Your room is not my room. However, what I can tell you is that if you move around your room clapping, you will hear reflections. If you play around with positioning your speakers differently, you will hear differences.

You can even go one step further and get a free software like Room EQ Wizard[38], a mic, and start studying your room hard: where are the bad spots? Where are the room modes? After what time delay do the first reflections reach my ears in this location? How about that location? Then build or buy some absorption panels, place them, and continue testing your room.

There are literally hundreds of pages and videos on how to build good absorbers; if I can do it, trust me, you can too. You will be amazed at what a couple of absorbers can change in terms of the quality of the listening experience.

I am short on resources; how do I get rid of reflections?
I can hear you grumbling: you do not have the time, it is too hard, etc. so I will start you off with the basics. We already know that your room is rectangular and that no one dimension is a multiple of another. The first idea is to get rid of the low-frequency modes closest to you, accumulating in angles and corners; this means panels first against corners with three walls (wall-wall-ceiling corners) then against corners with two walls (wall-wall angles)[39]. The next idea is to tame the earliest reflections. This means panels at the first reflection points for your speakers (both on the walls and on the ceiling!), then behind the speakers. If I had to choose your surface material for you, I would do plywood floors, mount 10 cm Foil Reinforced

---

[38] See [41]
[39] You can have a look at this very common Q&A from [42]

Kraft (FRK) rigid fiberglass panels at reflection points, then draperies or carpet on concrete at selected spots. Do not put too much carpet on your walls or your room will sound as dead as empty space and you must spend money on reverb plugins for your DAW!

There is a lot of literature both in books and on the internet which goes into a lot of detail about these topics[40]; my goal here is only to draw your attention to the fact that the listening environment is the most important factor to consider when building or analyzing a listening room. Yes, it is more important than which speakers or which cables are used in the signal chain.

This is of course also true when you are recording the sound: where you are recording it and how you are recording it is much more important than the microphones or the preamps used; one factor is even more important than where and how you record something: it is what you are recording; the performance quality trumps all the other factors. A great musician with a crappy mic will still always sound better than me on a Neumann.

4.4. Human Hearing

Sound is coming out of our speakers in our now well treated room. We know it does because our volume meter is pumping up and down. But why do we hear this sound? How is it possible that simple pressure changes in the air can transform into beautiful sounds?

Basic Hearing Mechanism

How does human hearing work?
This apparently simple phenomenon is in fact very complex. To give you an overview of the process, here is what happens (see the figure on the next page).

Air molecules moving back and forth under the varying pressure waves enter the external ear and travel to the *tympanic membrane* (also called *ear drum*; you pierced it when you forgot to bring your ear plugs to that Taiwanese trash metal concert you went to last month); the shape of the ear helps pressure waves concentrate into the ear canal. The membrane vibrates at the incoming sound frequencies and transmits them to the

---

[40] See [3], [17], [43] and [44]

middle ear, a cavity containing the three smallest bones in the human body (middle ear bones). The middle ear is there to do something we mentioned in Section 2.2: impedance matching! Impedance matching is needed at this stage because the inner ear is full of liquid while the external and middle ears are full of air; without impedance matching, pressure wave transmission would be too inefficient and the signal strength would be too faint to reach the brain.

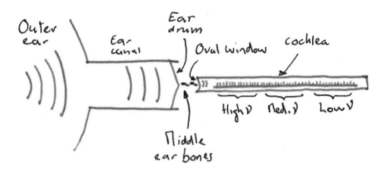

Figure 15 Human Hearing as a System [41]

Pressure is then transmitted from the middle ear to the inner ear through another membrane: the oval window. Instead of air pressure variations, we now have water pressure variations. Inside the inner ear is a long tube (the *cochlea*) which serves as a mechanic-neuro transducer: mechanical pressure (from the membrane moving back and forth) is transformed into electrical signals so that the brain can decode them. The tube inside the inner ear is built in such a fashion that at the entrance of the tube, high-frequency pressure waves are detected (through a resonance mechanism), while at the end of the tube, low-frequency vibrations are detected. Therefore, we can hear multiple frequencies simultaneously. Note that smell, taste and vision are chemical processes in nature; hearing, on the other hand, is fully mechanical.

---

[41] Reproduced with permission from [14]

From the Ear to the Brain

How does sound information get to the brain?

When pressure wave frequencies are detected alongside the tube, neurotransmitters are released into auditory nerve synapses found in the fibers connecting the nerve to the tube; neurotransmitter are chemicals acting as messengers between the different regions of a neuron. It is like a row of fireworks: depending on how long and how dry are the wicks, fireworks will fire off at different times at different points alongside the fireworks row.

Those synapses in turn produce electrical signals called action potentials which travel through the brainstem (found at the base of the brain at the end of the spinal cord) to the thalamus (found at the top of the brainstem) to the primary auditory cortex (part of the outer brain in which neurons' main function is to deal with auditory processing) in the temporal lobe (on the side of your head, where people aim their guns when their 10-hour mix session crashed and they never backed it up).

What is interesting is that the frequency specialization found in the regions of the tube inside the inner ear is also found in neurons connecting it to the auditory cortex: some neurons transmit certain frequencies better than others, depending on how they are connected to the tube. The common word for this transmission is "fire": neurons fire when they transmit information, making the fireworks image spot on ☺

Information such as pitch, timing and harmony is apparently generated in the auditory cortex. What happens after that is still a complete mystery. What is currently known is that information generated by the auditory cortex is transmitted to other parts of the brain for further processing. Of note is the fact that very low frequencies (below 20 Hz) can be sensed through touch rather than through hearing.

Psychoacoustics

How does our brain process the information?

Once the brain receives the encoded sound information, it processes it with cognitive brain functions studied in psychology and other human sciences. Thus, studying how sound is perceived is a multidisciplinary science at the crossroads between physics, biology, psychology and sociology called *psychoacoustics*.

Psychoacoustics is interesting because it shows us that hearing is not only complex from a biological standpoint, but also from a psychological (perception) standpoint. For example, if I listen to a sound missing its fundamental frequency but not its overtones, my brain will automatically extrapolate the sound's fundamental frequency from the overtones; this is the *missing fundamental* effect; in this case, our brain generates information that is not present in the incoming signal! This also happens with vision.

Sound localization is also calculated in the brain from very small differences in pitch, direction and volume. Another interesting psychoacoustical effect is *masking*, used to compress sound (see the Audio Bandwidth paragraph on page 63): when a louder sound source is heard simultaneously with a quieter sound source, the quieter source is masked and not perceived; thus, information encoding the frequencies from the quieter source can be omitted in the signal.

What is the Fletcher-Munson effect?

The king of all psychoacoustical effects is not an effect: the *Fletcher-Munson effect*, describes the fact that we do not hear all frequencies with the same loudness, even if the sound intensity is the same (see below). In other words, the curve describing the relationship between frequency (Hz) and loudness (dB) is not flat at all.

On the next picture, equal-loudness curves are shown for different sound intensities (measured in phons). Take the 40 phon curve: at 20 Hz, the sound is perceived to be very loud (90 dB), while at 1000 Hz it is only perceived to be 40 dB. Remember, a bump of 6 dB means twice the sound intensity. What is interesting is the bump between 1000 and 2000 Hz: an evolutionary biologist might say that our hearing system was selected because it could in fact perceive (and discriminate) human voice better than other systems because that frequency range is precisely where the human voice is centered; note how the loudness of the 1000-2000 Hz region is pretty on par with the corresponding sound intensity: 20 phon is about 20 dB loud, 40 phon is about 40 dB loud, etc.

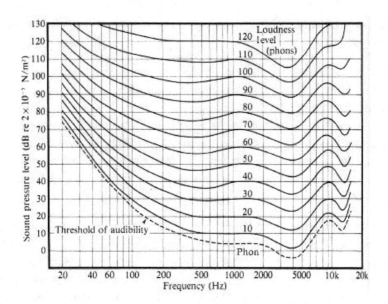

Figure 16 Fletcher-Munson Curves[42]

The Fletcher-Munson curves also explains why certain music sounds better when it is loud: all frequencies have a minimum loudness which ensures that they can be heard, giving the sound a fuller quality.

---

[42] Legally reproduced from [45]

Conclusion

So here we are. What a journey. The plucked string of page 12 has taken us through physics, electronics, computers, music, digital signal processing, acoustics, biology and psychology!

This is probably why audio is so fascinating: I would never have guessed the richness of the information I would find when I decided to write this book. I tried as hard as possible to give you correct information, or information that I could at least cross-check through a variety of sources. People in forums and even some of the books I have read give incorrect information, not because it is easy, but because it is hard: the underlying science is quite complex and not trivial at all; difficult mathematics get involved quickly so people take shortcuts or hearsay for the truth. This is especially apparent in electronics and acoustics. I do not pretend my book to be the ultimate answer; I did however make a conscious effort to seek out correct information.

I hope you enjoyed the ride as much as I did.

So now that we know all this, let us go make some music, shall we?

Appendix A: List of Sources

[1] Stéphane Pigeon. Audiocheck - Blind Testing a 10 kHz Upper Hearing Limit. [Online].
http://www.audiocheck.net/blindtests_frequency.php?frq=10

[2] Stéphane Pigeon. Audiocheck - Blind Testing a 20c Pitch Difference. [Online]. http://www.audiocheck.net/blindtests_pitch.php?cent=20

[3] Ethan Winer, *The Audio Expert*.: Elsevier Inc., 2012.

[4] Bobby Owsinski, *The Recording Engineer's Handbook*.: Course Technology, 2009.

[5] Matt McGlynn. Recording Hacks. [Online]. http://recordinghacks.com/microphones

[6] Bruce Bartlett. (2012, September) Pro Sound Web. [Online]. http://www.prosoundweb.com/article/size_matters_the_differences_in_large-_and_small-diaphragm_microphones/

[7] Wikipedia. Microphone. [Online]. http://en.wikipedia.org/wiki/Microphone

[8] William Beaty. (1995) Amasci. [Online]. http://www.amasci.com/amateur/transis.html

[9] Robjohns, Hugh. Sound On Sound. [Online]. https://web.archive.org/web/20150719032748/http://www.soundonsound.com/sos/jan03/articles/impedanceworkshop.asp

[10] Ray Rayburn. (2013) soundfirst.com. [Online]. http://www.soundfirst.com/xlr.html

[11] Al Keltz. Whirlwind. [Online]. http://whirlwindusa.com/support/tech-articles/high-and-low-impedance-signals/

[12] Mike Rivers. Mike Rivers Audio. [Online]. http://mikeriversaudio.files.wordpress.com/2010/10/micpreampsagain_updated.pdf

[13] Ciletti, Eddie. (2006, November) Mix Online. [Online]. http://mixonline.com/products/buyersguides/audio_microphone_preamplifier_technology/#online_extra_title

[14] Steven W. Smith, *The Scientist and Engineer's Guide to Digital Processing*. San Diego: California Technical Publishing, 1998.

[15] Yatri Trivedi. (2011, May) How To Geek. [Online]. http://www.howtogeek.com/64096/htg-explains-how-do-guitar-distortion-and-overdrive-work/

[16] The Engineering ToolBox. [Online]. http://www.engineeringtoolbox.com/accoustic-sound-absorption-d_68.html

[17] John Sayers' Recording Studio Design Forum. [Online].
http://www.johnlsayers.com/phpBB2/index.php

[18] Paul White. (2006, March) Sound On Sound. [Online].
http://www.soundonsound.com/sos/mar06/articles/usingreverb.htm

[19] Wikipedia. Timeline of Recordings With A Flanging Effect. [Online].
http://en.wikipedia.org/wiki/List_of_recordings_with_a_prominent_flanging
_effect

[20] Mike Senior. (2009, September) Sound On Sound. [Online].
http://www.soundonsound.com/sos/sep09/articles/classiccompressors.ht
m

[21] David Felton. (2012, November) Attack Magazine. [Online].
http://www.attackmagazine.com/features/top-20-best-hardware-
compressors-ever-made/

[22] National Instruments. (2015, May) Acquiring an Analog Signal:
Bandwidth, Nyquist Sampling Theorem, and Aliasing. [Online].
http://www.ni.com/white-paper/2709/en/

[23] Giorgio Pozzoli. (2004) TNT-Audio. [Online]. http://www.tnt-
audio.com/clinica/jitter1_e.html

[24] Rémy Fourré. (2004, August) Stereophile. [Online].
http://www.stereophile.com/reference/1093jitter/index.html

[25] Steinberg. The Cubase Line-up. [Online].
http://www.steinberg.net/en/products/cubase/line_up.html

[26] Ableton. Live Feature Comparison. [Online].
https://www.ableton.com/en/live/feature-comparison/

[27] Avid. Comparison. [Online]. http://www.avid.com/en/pro-tools/compare

[28] Cakewalk. Compare Versions. [Online].
http://www.cakewalk.com/Products/SONAR/Versions#start

[29] PreSonus. Compare Versions or Build Your Own. [Online].
http://www.presonus.com/products/Studio-One/Compare-Versions

[30] Tom Harris. (2001, February) How Stuff Works. [Online].
http://electronics.howstuffworks.com/speaker6.htm

[31] Chris Woodford. (2013, November) Headphones. [Online].
http://www.explainthatstuff.com/headphones.html

[32] Phil Ward. (2000, November) Sound On Sound. [Online].
http://www.soundonsound.com/sos/nov00/articles/ustandingmons.htm

[33] Mark T. A. Wieczorek. (2002, June) Mark T.A. Wieczorek. [Online].
http://www.marktaw.com/recording/Acoustics/AcousticsCrashCourse1-
Mod.html

[34] Don Davis, Eugene Patronis, and Pat Brown, *Sound System Engineering*, 4th ed. Burlington: Focal Press, 2013.

[35] Mark T. A. Wieczorek. (2002, June) Mark T. A. Wieczorek. [Online]. http://www.marktaw.com/recording/Acoustics/RoomModeStandingWaveCalcu.html

[36] Andy Melcher. amroc - the room mode calculator. [Online]. http://amroc.andymel.eu/

[37] Art Ludwig. Art Ludwig's Sound Page. [Online]. http://www.silcom.com/~aludwig/EARS.htm#Source_location

[38] Ethan Winer and Nyal Mellor. RealTraps - Room Measuring Series. [Online]. http://realtraps.com/art_measuring.htm#6

[39] Georgia State University. Hyperphysics. [Online]. http://hyperphysics.phy-astr.gsu.edu/hbase/Acoustic/revmod.html

[40] Bob Golds. Fiberglass, Rockwool, Polyester, Cotton, and Sheep Absorption Coefficients. [Online]. http://www.bobgolds.com/AbsorptionCoefficients.htm

[41] John Mulcahy. (2015) Room EQ Wizard. [Online]. http://www.roomeqwizard.com/

[42] Gearslutz. [Online]. https://www.gearslutz.com/board/bass-traps-acoustic-panels-foam-etc/125422-where-place-my-acoustic-panels.html

[43] Ethan Winer. (2009, November) RealTraps - Acoustics Basics. [Online]. http://realtraps.com/art_basics.htm

[44] Gearslutz Studio building / Acoustics forum. [Online]. http://www.gearslutz.com/board/studio-building-acoustics/

[45] StackExchange. Why should I use a logarithmic pot for audio applications? [Online]. http://electronics.stackexchange.com/questions/101191/why-should-i-use-a-logarithmic-pot-for-audio-applications

Appendix B: Units

The International System of units (SI) is founded on base 10 calculations. Not because we hate imperials; just because we have 10 fingers.

Here is a short list of the names covering the powers of ten used in this book.

Name	Abbr.	Scientific format	Decimal value	Example
micro	μ	10^{-6}	0,000001	1 μPa = 0,000001 Pa
milli	m	10^{-3}	0,001	1 mV = 0,001 V
deci	d	10^{-1}	0,1	1dB = 0,1 B
kilo	k	10^3	1000	1 kHz = 1000 Hz

Table 12 Common Powers of 10

Here are the basic units used in this book.

Name	Abbr.	SI equivalent	Measured value	Example
Ampère	A	A	Electric current	US toaster: 12,5 A
Bel	B	--	Sound intensity ratio	Human hearing threshold: 0 dB
Celsius	°C	°C	Temperature	Absolute zero: -273,15 °C
Fahrenheit	°F	1.8 °C + 32	Temperature	Normal body temperature: 98.6 °F
Foot	ft.	0.3048 m	Length, distance	Height of basketball rim: 10 ft.
Hertz	Hz	1 / s	Frequency	Middle C on a piano: 261.6 Hz
Inch	In.	0.0254 m	Length, distance	One foot is 12 inches
Ohm	Ω	$kg\ m^2 / s^3 / A^2$	Resistance, impedance	Copper wire 5 m long 2 mm^2 section: 0,04 Ω
Meter	m	m	Length, distance	Long jump world record: 8.95 m
Pascal	Pa	$kg / m / s^2$	Pressure	Atmospheric pressure: 1.01 kPa
Volt	V	$kg\ m^2 / s^3 / A$	Electric potential	Nerve cell resting potential: 75 mV

Table 13 Units Used in Audio Basics

Appendix C: Glossary

Appendix D: Tables, Figures and Equations

List of Tables

List of Figures

List of Equations

CPSIA information can be obtained
at www.ICGtesting.com
Printed in the USA
LVHW04s1745020818
585753LV00010B/874/P